A Practical and Insightful Journey through Counselling

An informative resource for clients, trainees and curious readers.

By

Jan Tilsley

MAPLE PUBLISHERS

A Practical and Insightful Journey through Counselling

Author: Jan Tilsley

ISBN 978-1-80723-143-9 (Paperback)
978-1-80723-144-6 (E-Book)

Book Layout and Book cover designed by:

White Magic Studios
whitemagicstudios.co.uk

Published by:
Maple Publishers
Fairbourne Drive, Atterbury,
Milton Keynes,
MK10 9RG, UK
www.maplepublishers.com

A CIP catalogue record for this title is available from the British Library.

For Mum

Who Always Believed In Me

Preface

This book developed out of numerous conversations with clients and colleagues, the result of which convinced me to create a resource that clarifies counselling, answers the questions many people are reluctant to ask, and offers information and confidence. I have a deep respect for counselling and for all the individuals who have allowed me to witness their resilience and courage.

If you are considering counselling or simply want to understand it better, this book is intended to guide you through the whole process, offering insight and awareness. I have drawn on theory, research, lived experience and personal reflections. My hope is that you will find encouragement and insight.

I have written this book to help people who are struggling with mental health issues and to guide them through the counselling process toward psychological well-being. I am a qualified counsellor with over 30 years of experience working with individuals from all walks of life. My academic background includes a BSc in Psychology, a PGCE, and diplomas in Counselling, Supervision, Group Analysis and Hypnotherapy. Over the years, I have taught counselling, supervised counsellors, and held positions as both a moderator and examiner roles that have enabled a deeper understanding of the profession and its challenges. My strengths lie in groupwork and private practice, and my career has included lectures in private settings, community services and mental health organisations. All these experiences have given me a profound appreciation for the courage it takes to begin counselling.

Through these pages, I aim to share awareness, professional knowledge and practical insights. I hope these words will prompt curiosity, offer new thinking and unlock possibilities. My thanks go to clients, my mentor and colleagues, who have all inspired me throughout my counselling career.

Thank you for picking up this book. I hope it serves as a gentle companion on your counselling journey.

CONTENTS

Introduction

'Your counselling journey will begin with a single step. Let this be yours'

To counselling clients, trainee counsellors and curious readers.

There are different titles given to those who help people with their issues and concerns: therapist, counsellor, psychotherapist, and practitioner. I will use counsellor and counselling throughout.

This book has been written to provide you with a practical and comprehensive guide to counselling, grounded in empathy, ethics, and evidence. Its aim is to help you understand counselling and what it entails. It will offer you the reality, the whole story, including the good and the positive, as well as the imperfect and the ineffective. You, the clients, are the most important people in the whole of the counselling profession. You deserve to know what is involved in all aspects of counselling and, above all, you are entitled to the highest professional standard of counselling for your welfare and psychological health.

Many people come to counselling with little idea as to what it is, what it can offer and whether it is right for them. It is normal to feel indecisive; however, counselling will make space for your questions, your hopes and fears, and it will all be heard without judgment. This book will guide you through the elements of counselling, looking at the whole process, what you can expect and how to benefit the most from it.

A substantial number of books have been written about counselling, and in the main, they have all been written for counsellors. This book is different; I have written it for you, the most significant people in the entire counselling process, some of whom, I believe, have not been sufficiently acknowledged or appreciated. My personal experiences, professional insight, and commitment to the counselling profession have inspired me to write this book and to share it with you.

The following chapters will take you on a journey through counselling, where you will be offered information and insight, an opportunity to gain awareness and understanding about all the ins and outs and whys and wherefores of counselling. This will enable you to make informed and conscious choices in relation to the type of counselling and counsellor that will be best suited for you. Each chapter will offer explanations of what counselling is, its process and procedures, finding good counsellors, what to do if you are concerned and what to expect from counselling sessions. I also share the counselling profession, which is made up of a number of different sectors and many people in varied roles. Together with a brief look into the inner workings of the counselling profession as a whole. The book presents gentle challenges and sheds light on hidden aspects. It provides practical information and inspires you to think deeply and consider each chapter carefully.

Personal Reflection.

My first experience of counselling, decades ago as a client, was unsettling, poorly managed, without boundaries and with no contract. *I felt confused and distressed, especially when the counsellor sat in silence. Instead of feeling supported, I left feeling worse.*

Looking back, it was an ordeal I would not wish on anyone. However, this experience planted a seed. Years later, it motivated me to become a counsellor. I wanted to offer the safe, empathic, compassionate space that I had needed but had never received.

Three years of training and a psychology degree helped me achieve my goal. What began as an unpleasant experience became the foundation for a career built on integrity, commitment and respect.

This thought-provoking book will provide information and guidance related to all things counselling, it will offer a peek into the grey areas and a glimpse at its meaningful benefits. The very nature of counselling is based on openness and integrity, genuineness and respect, yet in the face of this, counselling has its weaknesses and imperfections. I have written every page with you in mind, to offer insight, perception and knowledge. I include a series of reflections taken from my own experiences, all true and enlightening. They are not case studies; they merely summarise personal reflections from my professional work. They highlight challenges and rights and wrongs. I am sharing them to offer awareness of the differing ethical standards counsellors may have. We will further explore the foundations of counselling, its process, the professional relationship, and the theoretical approaches that shape the work. I invite you to read this book with an open mind.

This book is for you, especially if you have ever felt or may feel the power of empathy or the courage it takes to ask for help. May it offer insight, comfort and assurance.

Chapter One
Setting The Scene

The Path to Insight

'The route to awareness is seldom straight. It strolls through consciousness, feelings, and thoughts.'

Counselling has a fascinating history that can be traced back to philosophers like Aristotle and Socrates, who established the groundwork for personal growth and self-reflection. Moving on to the late 19th and early 20th centuries, Sigmund Freud appears as a pioneering thinker with his innovative psychoanalysis. Further advancements arrived with Alfred Adler and Carl Jung, who developed Freud's ideas. Counselling took a significant remodel with Abraham Maslow and Carl Rogers, innovators who significantly transformed counselling, highlighting human potential and psychological health using client-centred counselling. After World War two counselling advanced; it was a valuable comfort for soldiers' psychological trauma. Counselling has now developed into a substantial helping profession, answering the needs of many and their emotional health and well-being.

It sits comfortably within the mental health professions, albeit at the very bottom of the hierarchy.

Psychiatrists are medical doctors qualified and specialised in mental illness. In the main, they diagnose, manage and treat people with mental illness, often with medication and tend to work with severe conditions. They will have had many years of study as a doctor and many more to become a psychiatrist.

Psychologists will have had a minimum of six years of study at university and will be qualified at a Doctorate or Master's level. Some are clinical psychologists who are trained in assessing, evaluating, diagnosing and treating mental illness. Others are counselling psychologists, helping people to cope with stress and emotional issues. Some may work in research or in academic settings.

Psychotherapists often work with clients for longer periods of time and with deeper psychological issues. They may offer more than one session a week to clients. Their treatment plans can be fairly complex, utilising specialised psychotherapeutic approaches. Their training may be between three and six years.

Counsellors work with clients to help with emotional distress and often on a short-term basis. Their training is at Diploma level, usually three years part-time, which enables them to help with many client issues, using therapeutic approaches.

There is some similarity between counsellors and psychotherapists. They have many common factors but also some distinct differences. The names counsellor and psychotherapist are not legally recognised and, as such, anyone can call themselves a counsellor or a psychotherapist. Both are considered talking therapies, and both work with clients' distressing and life-challenging issues. The relationship with clients is especially important for both, but psychotherapy goes deeper than counselling by delving into the past. Counselling is more behaviour focussed and deals with the present. Their training and theoretical approaches differ, but they both, in their own ways, help clients.

Reflecting on the qualifications of the other mental health workers, counselling has the lowest qualification. Irrespective of this, counselling can be immensely helpful for many clients; it can help to reduce the symptoms of many mental health worries; however, it may not benefit all clients.

The standard of counselling you receive is very much determined by the counsellor themselves, the training they have attained, and their counselling experience. Not all counsellor training is the same, and some is substandard. A counsellor's experience of counselling will differ considerably. Not everyone who wants to be a counsellor will have what it takes. You should expect high standards from counsellors who must be professional and ethical, offer clear boundaries and have a good knowledge base of theory and skills.

The Counselling Profession.

The counselling profession is huge, and most aspects of it are centred around counsellors. It is a profession that has grown substantially over just a few decades since it became accepted as a recognised intervention for mental health issues. Within today's society, the rapid growth of counselling attempts to satisfy the demands of an increasing population. A population where many feel the stresses, pressures, and emotional distress from living in a fast-paced, technologically advanced and consumerist world. The profession begins with the need for counsellors, but counsellors need to be trained, and so training organisations appear in further and higher education and in the private sector. A qualification must be achieved, and so the number of awarding bodies increases to offer qualifications. Professionals decide that the counselling industry needs to be overseen in terms of knowledge and skills, as well as good practice and conduct, and so professional counselling bodies emerge. Counsellors need regular mentoring to ensure that they are working in a safe and ethical manner and are keeping up to date with current developments, and so counselling supervisors are necessary, who also need to be trained. Counsellors must maintain their continued professional development, which means that various organisations pop up to meet these requirements, offering lectures, workshops, and courses. Counselling journals, books and online information also become a part of the industry, and so it continues.

The profession produces a considerable number of counsellors, but the competence of some is often diluted due to awarding bodies concentrating on quantity over quality. This is worrying, as many of these counsellors are not sufficiently qualified, which then affects the standard of counselling offered. You, as clients, uphold the entire infrastructure of counselling and are essential to the profession. You deserve the absolute best from both counsellors and the counselling process. You need to fully understand what counselling entails and be aware that a small number of counsellors will fail to help you to appreciate what counselling is and what it involves. You must be given the facts, the details, and clear explanations about both counselling and your counsellor.

What is Counselling?

The term 'counselling' is especially vague; it is a generic term used throughout the counselling profession, yet it remains blurry and, at times, contentious. There are as many definitions of counselling as there are books written on the subject, and there are many thousands of books on counselling. Each definition presents the author's point of view and the intended audience. For many, counselling means very different things, including a large variety of methods, theories and contexts. Unfortunately, dictionary definitions often associate counselling with advice giving, which contradicts counselling principles. In practice, offering advice is unethical and should always be avoided.

Among many professional counsellors, there is no approved definition of counselling. However, counsellors have a responsibility to make certain that clients clearly understand what counselling involves and how sessions progress. In counselling, the professional therapeutic relationship offers a safe, confidential space for you. It is about facilitating self-awareness, psychological healing, and personal growth. It is a process in which a trained counsellor helps you to explore and understand your feelings, thoughts, and behaviours. It provides an opportunity for you to discuss your concerns and any issues you may be facing. The aim is to help you gain insight, find new perspectives, and develop coping strategies to improve your overall well-being. Counsellors enable you to express yourself without fear of being judged. They ask thoughtful questions and help you to uncover patterns, beliefs, and emotions that may be influencing your well-being. It also helps you understand your thoughts and feelings about your issues and yourself. It enables you to change your thinking, emotional responses, and behaviour, and to grow and develop. It can help you uncover hidden strengths, and resources to deal with your issues. You should feel supported, helped to clarify your issues, encouraged to reflect and express your feelings, and empowered by the process.

While counselling can be life-changing for many, it should be carefully considered. The profession has its limitations. It is not a magic fix and is not protected from the challenges that affect and influence the profession. Many counsellors are skilled and empathic, but others may lack the experience which is indispensable for working with clients. Not all counsellors gel with all clients; a good match is essential, as a poor match will do more harm than good.

Mental Health.

Mental health refers to our emotional, psychological, and social well-being. It enables us to cope with life, to learn and work. It has an effect on how we think, feel, and behave, and it influences how we handle stress and relate to others. Good mental health gives us the strength to cope with life's challenges. Mental health affects all of us, all ages, backgrounds and walks of life. It is experienced differently by each individual one of us. Mental health can be associated with distress and risk of harm.

Your mental health matters, and it takes courage to ask for help. Good mental health will enable confidence and self-worth.

Benefits of Counselling.

Counselling offers many valuable benefits, with emotional support being one of the most significant, where clients feel heard and understood. Counselling is empowering, helping to build confidence. Issues with relationships, communication and interpersonal skills can be helped through making better connections with others. Counselling promotes self-esteem, self-acceptance, and self-awareness. It provides you with coping strategies and stress management techniques to support your mental well-being. Counselling can assist in helping you to gain insight into your issue(s) and enhance decision-making. If you are feeling overwhelmed, confused or despondent, then consider speaking to a counsellor who could offer the support and professional help that you need.

Counselling and its limitations.

Counselling can certainly be beneficial, but it is important to acknowledge that it has its limitations and cannot always help all clients. It is not a 'cure all' and may result in client nervousness, changes in relationships, careers and significant life events. Counselling can be expensive and requires commitment to regular sessions. It is not a quick fix with immediate solutions; it takes time and resolution. It has its challenges, and clients may feel worse before they feel any progress. Counsellors who lack cultural sensitivity can create barriers to effective counselling. Some therapeutic approaches may not be productive for every client.

Finding a good counsellor who understands your needs is most important; a mismatch will block any progress. Counselling may not be sufficient for all clients; some mental health conditions, such as severe depression, bipolar disorder, or schizophrenia, often require other therapeutic approaches, which may include medications and psychiatric care.

Different Types of Counselling.

Individual counselling is the most popular and widely used form of counselling, where you work with a counsellor on a one-on-one basis. The counsellor focuses completely on your needs and issues.

Couples counselling is for clients with relationship issues, where both parties work together with a counsellor to improve communication and connectedness.

Family counselling, as the name implies, is where families work together with a counsellor. Usually, this would address family issues such as conflicts and dynamics.

Group counselling is often based on support for a number of people who work with a counsellor together to share experiences.

Specialised counselling concentrates on one specific counselling issue, for example, addictions, trauma, substance abuse, or hoarding disorder.

Does Counselling Work?

My immediate response is that counselling can be very effective, but it is subject to individual circumstances. Counselling offers a safe space to explore thoughts, feelings, and experiences, and for many, it leads to greater self-awareness. However, it is not magic; it takes time, trust, and an inclination to engage. The relationship between the counsellor and the client is essential; when that interaction feels comfortable, progress can happen.

If you persevere, counselling can be all-encompassing. Counselling is supportive, enabling growth and moving forward. Subsequently, the short answer is yes, counselling can work. However, the longer answer is more complex. Counselling is not a instant solution, and not every approach works for everyone. There is no real, definite answer. On the one hand, theoretically speaking, it is counselling research that may help with the answer. On the other hand, practically speaking, it is more about the actual counsellor and the counselling that is on offer. The benefits of counselling have always been contentious and difficult to prove. The debate about its usefulness has been ongoing for decades. The truth no doubt lies somewhere between counselling being helpful and not helpful. Many counsellors and clients believe it is beneficial, and the profession promotes the idea that counselling works for all issues and all clients, maintaining its popularity, growth, and profitability. As such, the question of its helpfulness is transferred to researchers. However, most counselling researchers work within the industry, and it is naturally in their interest to prove its usefulness. Counselling research involves a number of factors and much deliberation before conclusions can be reached. Research seems to be the only way to confirm counselling's effectiveness. Research demonstrates accountability and credibility, which, in turn, offers clients confidence and assurance, provided the results are positive!

The efficacy of counselling research has been brought into question by a number of emotionless people within the counselling profession. They actually suggest that such research is not really worth the effort and have stated that counselling research is trying to 'quantify the unquantifiable.' Strangely, very little research has been carried out on the negative effects of counselling and even less on the expertise of counsellors. Ethical considerations make counselling research complicated. The confidential nature of counselling and the outcomes for clients suggest that research must be given careful consideration. Research also suggests that many aspects are subject to change, and these will influence the outcome of the research. There is a huge question mark over the validity of counselling research. Statistically, it may be important, but in terms of practice, it is, more often than not, worthless. With an increasing demand for mental health services, more counsellors are needed; however, not all counsellors are competent and do not maintain high standards, giving rise to poor care. Prioritising quantity over quality is an important issue as it can have serious consequences for clients. The counselling profession must be certain that counsellors beginning their career are well trained, skilled, competent and can offer high-quality care to clients

Personal Reflection.

During my time in counselling, I have witnessed situations that left me very unsettled*, sessions where counsellors failed to listen empathically, and where counsellors disregarded client concerns. I recall one instance where a vulnerable client was met with coldness, leaving the client more confused and isolated than before the session. Such experiences are not only distressing, but they are also harmful.*

Conversely, I have observed counsellors who have been competent, professional, caring, respectful, empathic, ethical, and understanding. These counsellors support clients and enable progress. They facilitate and empower clients and establish a climate that is beneficial for growth and healing. These are the counsellors that you need to look for.

Counselling supports mental health; however, it has its defects and weaknesses. I would never discourage anyone from seeking help; quite the opposite. Even so, be aware that counselling can take time, costs can vary, you may face uncomfortable emotions, and cultural differences may not be understood by the counsellor. Counselling's weaknesses and limitations need to be taken into consideration. Asking questions and being informed will empower you to make the right choices for your mental health and to look for support that genuinely meets your needs. Sometimes the counselling may not be flawless, but it may still be really helpful.

Chapter Two
What Defines A Counsellor

The essence of the role

'A counsellor does not fix problems, but facilitates change and well-being.'

Clients who choose to engage in counselling make a courageous decision and a significant commitment. It is not always easy to disclose personal thoughts, feelings, experiences, and issues to a stranger who shares nothing of themselves with you. Counsellors are, for you, unfamiliar people to whom you give your trust and confidence, and with whom you enter into an intimate, professional working relationship.

Who are Counsellors?

Counsellors are compassionate people who work to help others with emotional, psychological, and relational issues. Their professional training enables them to listen deeply, empathise, offer no judgment, and create a safe space for clients. Their work is based on trust, patience, and a genuine desire to support clients through their counselling journey. Most counsellors are generally resilient and good listeners. Many keep their own lives quite private. They have hobbies, and some have families; they watch television and are susceptible to having bad days and the ups and downs of life. Outside of their counselling roles, they are the same as anyone else. Some often seek support for themselves. While counsellors may have many similarities, they come from all walks of life. Some have been teachers, nurses, social workers or had successful business careers. What connects them is their dedication to helping and supporting others to enable healing.

Why become a counsellor?

The people who choose to become counsellors are often very motivated, mature and have had life experiences. Some wish to support people through their issues, whilst others have had their own challenges, which influences them to help others. A few have a great interest in psychology or want a career that is meaningful, where they can bring about change. Counselling intrigues many who are curious to know more about it. Trainees who enter counselling training often does not realise that it entails a huge commitment and responsibility. Counsellor training is often difficult and underestimated by those trainees who do not possess the required skills. It is challenging, demanding and often draining. A number will leave the course at this stage, whilst others will continue on the course to enhance their existing careers or for personal growth. Those trainees who complete the course are usually the ones who become practising counsellors.

Professional Qualifications.

A counsellor is more than a professional helper; they are trained, ethical, and compassionate; they support clients through emotional and psychological distress by facilitating growth and self-understanding. Counsellors are typically trained at a diploma level in further education or private training organisations. Some choose more formal training in psychology or psychotherapy at a degree or postgraduate level.

Once qualified counsellors should register and become accredited with professional bodies which confirm the counsellors' training and ensure that they work according to their standards of practice and ethics, including regular supervision and professional development.

Counsellor competences.

- Actively listen, non-judgmental, empathic.
- Adhere to boundaries to maintain a safe and professional relationship.
- Self-awareness to appreciate their own emotional responses.
- Confidentiality by protecting the client's privacy.
- Support and facilitate change.
- Culturally sensitive, supporting difference and diversity.
- Ethical and accountable. Understand and value clients.

Personal Reflection.

During my career, I have known many counsellors and encountered a large number who are genuinely good, caring, empathic, and committed. *Unfortunately, I have also come across mediocre counsellors, and some who, in my view, should not be practising at all. I have seen first-hand how the quality of counsellors can vary, and how this affects the counselling and the outcomes for clients. Whilst many counsellors are professional, accomplished, and proficient in helping many clients with their issues, not all are competent. They are often unaware of their own limitations and lack sufficient knowledge of theoretical approaches and practical skills. My work as a counselling trainer enabled me to recognise students who showed real potential to become effective counsellors, and also to support those who were not as knowledgeable. Sadly, some of these trainees did not possess the qualities required to meet the standard, even after numerous additional learning support sessions. I found it quite disheartening when they were unable to progress, and to ease their disappointment, I would meet with them as a group to explore alternative paths and options that may still allow them* *to help others in meaningful ways. Not everyone who wishes to become a counsellor will make the grade, and that is a difficult but important truth.*

The concept of the wounded healer.

Introduced by Swiss psychiatrist Carl Jung, who suggested that people who have experienced and, in part, resolved their own emotional issues are capable of helping others. Jung and psychiatrist Irvin Yalom agreed that only those who have been 'wounded' themselves can really heal. This concept has been associated with counselling; it may also apply to professions such as medicine and teaching, for example. Many counsellors who have a desire to help have been influenced by this concept based on their own experiences of distress. Although the theory holds emotional influence, I am undecided. Research on the wounded healer is limited, making it difficult to offer any conclusions. In practice, undetermined personal issues can cause a breach of boundaries, such as counsellors self-disclosing, which is of no help to the client. I have been aware of aspects of the wounded healer in many of my students; some have become exceptional counsellors, while others have struggled. I continue to sit on the fence, in the hope that counsellors will consider this theory with caution.

What do Counsellors do?

Counsellors create a safe, confidential space where clients can speak freely without fear of being judged. They ask meaningful questions to enable clients to consider their thoughts, feelings, and behaviours. They offer emotional support and empathy, together with facilitating personal growth through self-awareness and confidence. Counsellors work in many different ways, but they all help clients with a wide range of issues, from stress, depression, and anxiety to loss, relationship difficulties and addictions. Some counsellors work with a variety of issues, while others choose to specialise in areas such as marriage guidance, substance misuse, or obsessive-compulsive disorders.

The skills and interventions used will depend on the counsellor's therapeutic approach. The counselling process itself varies and is modified to suit each individual client and the specific issues they bring. Clients are always in the 'driving seat', while the counsellor uses different strategies and techniques to support you through the therapeutic relationship. Counsellors must begin by developing a strong therapeutic relationship; without it, no real progress can be made. Skills are used to support you, including facilitating awareness, deepening understanding and enabling insight so that choices and changes can be considered. Emotions and experiences, thoughts and feelings will be examined and discussed, all with the counsellor using care, empathy and compassion.

What defines a counsellor?

Personal Qualities

- Empathy and patience. Sincerity and integrity.
- Strong communication skills. Resilience and fairness.
- Emotional intelligence. Wisdom and courage.
- Cultural sensitivity. Competence and assertiveness.
- Commitment and ethics. Listening and understanding.
- Calm and non-judgmental. Self-awareness and knowledge.
- Motivation and life experience. Respect and humility.

Skills

- ➢ Open questions. Confronting.
- ➢ Immediacy. Non-verbal appreciation.
- ➢ Elaboration. Problem solving.
- ➢ Paraphrasing. Summarising.
- ➢ Reflecting. Active listening.
- ➢ Building rapport. Facilitating.

Calibre of Counsellors.

The calibre of a counsellor can make a huge difference in the counselling interaction. It varies considerably as to whether counsellors can deliver exactly what clients need. It is dependent upon several factors, from the counsellor's ability, the training they have received, their experience of counselling, competency, knowledge, and expertise. A good counsellor will attempt to offer an approach and a way of working to suit each individual client's needs. Exactly what a client needs will depend on the actual issue(s) brought to counselling.

Foundational Counsellors - Newly qualified or early-career professionals.

Competent Practitioners - Mid-level experience, typically a few years in. Highly Skilled Counsellors-Seasoned professionals with much clinical insight.

Master-Level Counsellors - Often supervisors or trainers.

The calibre of counsellors can further be influenced by the following.

Training & Credentials - some counsellors may have advanced degrees or diplomas. Cultural Competence - the ability to understand backgrounds and respect difference. Personal

Maturity - sometimes, life experience and emotional depth play a big role.

Professional competence is essential to have knowledge of theories and practices.

Personal attributes are also important, such as resilience, showing empathy and compassion, non-judgemental and offering trust and rapport.

The very best counsellors will show integrity, insight and skill. Knowing whether a counsellor is good is essential. Unfortunately, many counsellors fall under the umbrella of being 'good enough,' a term often used in the counselling profession. Defining 'good enough' for counsellors is an impossible task. To me, 'good enough' does not mean 'good.' As 'good' signifies competence, 'good enough' merely suggests being average. I know which type of counsellor I would choose!

A mediocre counsellor might not be completely inadequate, but could make poor choices and decisions. A poor counsellor who is below standard could engage in unsafe practices, leading to harmful outcomes for clients. Good counsellors are filled with compassion, a wealth of patience, and a good deal of resilience. Skilled counsellors are knowledgeable in theories, accomplished in skills and professional in practice. Their calibre should not just be evaluated by their qualifications but rather by the intensity of their presence. There are many good counsellors who can help you with your issues. Keep looking until you find one who is truly right for you.

Chapter Three

A Needle In A Haystack

Finding a good counsellor

'In a room full of voices, the right one does not speak louder but listens better'

The Search.

It can be difficult to find a good counsellor, one who is capable, confident, and continually striving to improve. In your search, always ensure that good counsellors are registered with a professional body; this shows that they are committed to maintaining important ethical standards. However, finding such a counsellor can be an arduous task that takes time, effort, and determination. When you are struggling and feeling stressed with issues you want to resolve, the task becomes even harder. Finding a good counsellor will involve internet browsing and/or phone calls or messages/emails, but it will be time well spent. To find a counsellor who is right for you will require a conversation with the counsellor and a precounselling session, the latter being something that not all counsellors offer.

Personal Reflection.

Throughout my practice, I have always offered potential clients a pre-counselling session of around twenty to thirty minutes. *This time allows us to discuss the client's concerns and what counselling might involve, and begin to establish a sense of safety and trust. I share my experience and qualifications, answer any questions,* *and introduce the counselling contract. It is a space where the client can begin to feel heard without pressure or commitment.*

I have found these sessions to be very beneficial. They offer a short break before the therapeutic journey begins, giving clients the time to reflect and decide whether they feel ready to proceed. For me, it is also a moment to consider whether I am the right person to support them.

This initial meeting is a useful beginning. It can ease anxiety and clarify expectations. It can be held face-to-face, over the phone, or via video call.

Over the years, many clients have expressed how useful this session was. Some have said it helped them feel less anxious and more informed. This preparation can be really significant for the therapeutic relationship.

If you can pay for your counselling, you have the best chance of finding a counsellor who is a good fit for you. If you are not in a position to find and pay for a good counsellor, you will probably not be able to choose one as a counsellor will be allocated to you. General practitioners' surgeries have their own counsellors, and voluntary organisations typically have several counsellors with varying levels of ability and experience. Voluntary organisations are often free or offer reduced rates, with some requesting a donation or operating on a sliding scale based on your income and ability to pay. Some voluntary organisations provide counselling for specific issues such as domestic violence, sexual abuse, or bereavement, while others offer more general support. Voluntary organisations and some general practitioner surgeries may also have trainee counsellors in their final year of training, which you should be aware of. While some trainee counsellors are very capable, not all are proficient. Receiving counselling from a trainee counsellor should always be a choice that you make. Waiting lists for counsellors in voluntary organisations and general practitioner surgeries are often quite long, less so for private counsellors, where you have to pay.

In addition to voluntary counselling organisations or your general practitioner's surgery, you can self-refer to the National Health Service, which offers free counselling for a limited number of sessions. Your general practitioner can assist you with a National Health Service referral. This counselling may be face-to-face or, for certain issues, delivered via an online programme. The National Health Service counselling service is called Psychological Therapies, and you can refer yourself online or visit your general practitioner's surgery for help. The service will contact you to discuss your concerns and determine what type of counselling would be most suitable. The main form of counselling offered by Psychological Therapies is cognitive behavioural therapy, including online programmes for guided self-help. However, other types of counselling may also be available. National Health Service sessions are usually limited to between six and twelve, and waiting lists are often very long, about four to eighteen weeks. They deal mainly with anxiety, stress and depression and not so much with deeper issues. You would not be able to choose your counsellor.

Another available option would be employee-assisted programme services. It is useful to check with your employer if you are working, as many employers use these services. They are employee support schemes offered to employees with issues that may be affecting work performance or health. In the main, there is no charge to the employee, but sessions may be limited. All the counsellors that they use are qualified, experienced and accredited. The standards of confidentiality and privacy are strictly adhered to. Schools, colleges, and universities will have their own counselling department for both students and staff.

It may be that you cannot afford counselling, or perhaps you do not have an internet connection. No matter what your situation is, if you are struggling with issues or mental health, then consider the following: Libraries have computers that are free to use and many self-help books on mental health and well-being. There are also online apps that could help you, provided that you have the internet or a mobile phone. The National Health Service have mental health and well-being apps for teens and adults. All these are worth considering and may be able to help you. In addition, if you are on a huge waiting list for counselling or, for whatever reason, cannot arrange to see a counsellor, either private or through an organisation, then you may consider visiting a drop-in centre. Your doctor's surgery or library may be able to point you in the right direction, or Citizens Advice can help you to find one. You will be able to have a friendly and non-judgemental discussion and receive support from trained helpers. Be certain to check their times, and if you have a phone, then phone them beforehand to make an appointment.

Another option to consider is joining a support group where people with a similar issue to yourself get together and encourage and help each other. They are usually part of local charities and libraries. Citizens Advice and your local council can help you to choose a group that matches your needs.

Private counsellors enable you to book directly with them, and you would have a choice of days and times, including weekends and evenings. Their waiting times are usually one to seven days on average. They generally work with most issues, and you can choose your counsellor. They also offer longer-term counselling. Be aware of private counsellors who do not belong to a professional body or who are not accredited.

How to find a Counsellor.

It is always worth checking with friends, colleagues and family members for counsellor recommendations, bearing in mind that they may have been a good fit for your cousin or friend, but there is no guarantee that they will be right for you. Many counsellors will advertise locally in monthly publications, and these may be worth considering. The main place to look for a counsellor is online through counselling directories. Professional counselling bodies often have a directory of counsellors. British Association for Counselling and Psychotherapy, United Kingdom Council for Psychotherapy, British Psychological Society and National Counselling and Psychotherapy Society. There are other counselling directories online, and all are worth checking out. A counsellor who is in the directory of a professional body must be either a registered and/or accredited member. Each counsellor will state what they specialise in, the cost for their services, something about themselves, their therapeutic approach and their availability.

The cost of Counselling.

If you are able to pay for a private counsellor, then it may be useful to check your budget, given that the costs of private counselling vary and can be from thirty-five pounds to one hundred and fifty pounds, plus, for each session, on average, about forty to eighty pounds. Online counselling may be less, averaging around thirty pounds to ninety-five pounds, plus for each session. Some counsellors may work on a sliding scale dependent upon your income. Most counsellors work on a minimum of six sessions. A small number of counsellors may even offer a limited number of pro bono (free) sessions. Private counsellors will not only vary in their fees and the number of sessions offered but also in their therapeutic approaches. Take care to ensure that the counsellor is fully qualified, registered, experienced and accredited. Some, just out of training, counsellors will set up in private practice with little experience, and be aware of these even if they offer reduced price sessions.

Counsellors with considerable qualifications and experience may charge more money. Counsellors in affluent areas may charge clients more than those in less affluent areas. Those with more overheads, such as a large office, a receptionist and client seating areas, toilets and a coffee machine will charge more than a counsellor who simply rents a single room. Even a counsellor in a simple private room will have overheads to pay and have to charge a reasonable amount for their services to cover their outgoing costs. They will receive a lot less than they are paid after covering their expenses. It may be useful to shop around for lower cost options, but take care that the counsellor is qualified, competent and professional.

Counselling children and young people.

Counsellors working with children and young people need to have had specialised training and a counselling qualification in order to appreciate the challenges and developmental needs of this age group. They should have a clear appreciation of the social development stages, together with an understanding of emotional and psychological advancement. Safe guarding and child protection awareness are crucial, as well as a knowledge of mental health issues that affect young people. An understanding of specialised techniques related to children and young people and their application is also essential. A respect for diversity and effective age-appropriate communication is paramount. Exploring the relationship and family dynamics between children and young people and their parents and carers is necessary, as is parents' support and care. Counsellors working with children and young people can make errors that will affect the quality of support provided. Common mistakes include using inappropriate techniques or language, and failing to adjust to the child's developmental stage and rushing the process without considering the child's environment and family dynamics, all of which can have a negative impact. However, when a counsellor is properly trained, self-aware, and receives regular supervision, such mistakes are less likely to occur. Always take the time to verify a counsellor's qualifications. Counsellors for children and young people can offer psychological and emotional support appropriate for developmental stages, from ages four to eighteen. Children and adolescents can discuss their experiences, such as family, self-harm, anxiety and stress. These counsellors need to be qualified and knowledgeable.

What do you want from counselling and a counsellor?

I would strongly recommend taking some time to look carefully for your counsellor. However, before you begin your search, ensure that the time is right for you to commence counselling. Ask yourself if you are ready to open up to a counsellor and share personal details, to explore your feelings and to learn about yourself and possibly change some thoughts and behaviours. Indications that you may not be ready are a lack of motivation and feeling that counselling may be a chore, thoughts that counselling will not be helpful or being afraid of making changes. Check also that there is nothing else that you may need help with first, such as practical, physical or legal help. If you are ready for counselling, then it is really useful to start making a note, just a couple of words on each of the following examples, to help you to find a counsellor who is right for you.

What do you want to achieve from counselling? - to feel less stressed, to overcome your anxiety, to make important decisions, to repair a relationship.

What do you want from a counsellor? - to sort out your confusion, to deal with feelings, to teach you skills, to help you to understand yourself, to provide structure.

What would you like in a counsellor? - a counsellor who is practical and down to earth, one who will really listen and offer support, one who will understand, one who is caring and empathic.

It will also be helpful to clarify –

Whether you want a counsellor of a specific gender or gender identity, perhaps you do not mind or it may be important to you and the issues you will be working on to choose a male or female.

Perhaps you need a counsellor who understands your language and culture – or just an interpreter.

A counsellor who is older than you or younger - this may or may not be important to you.

A counsellor who will understand your disability – one who is competent and can discuss your needs.

One in your local area or further afield - if travelling is an issue, then travelling to a local counsellor would be easier. You may feel more comfortable with a counsellor who lives and works a distance from where you live and work.

Consider also -

How do you want to work with a counsellor - Face to face or video call, telephone or email? Video calls are popular and more available. Personally, I would suggest that there is nothing better than face-to-face counselling, but I appreciate that some people may have difficulty in talking face to face for a variety of reasons. There are also some people who are not mobile or who are unable to leave their homes and travel to a counselling venue. Whatever the reason for choosing email, telephone, or video call, it is essential to check privacy settings and take care when giving personal details, use secure passwords and ensure that you have privacy in your own home for your sessions.

Following on from these preliminaries, it is always beneficial to talk to prospective counsellors before the counselling begins. This may not be possible for the National Health Service or voluntary organisations. The organisations themselves may contact you with a date for your first session, and if this is the case, then take this opportunity to ask anything that you want to know about the counsellor and the counselling at your first session. It may be the counsellor themselves who will phone you to make an appointment, which is ideal for checking out anything that you are unsure about. If the appointment is emailed to you, then it is fine to respond with your queries. Finding out some basic things about your counsellor and the counselling will help to put you at ease, and if you speak with the counsellor on the phone, then this will help with beginning to develop a therapeutic relationship. Some counsellors will have assessment sessions with clients. However, in voluntary organisations, some assessment sessions may be carried out by people other than the counsellor.

It is important, when looking for a private counsellor, to choose several from the directories and read their profiles, theoretical approach, specialities and fees. Choose at least three to phone who, on paper, seem to match your requirements. This will help you to get a feel for them and will enable you to ask all that you need to know and are unsure about.

Be aware that good counsellors must uphold boundaries and maintain a professional and therapeutic distance. They must also not only listen to you but actually hear what you are sharing.

I have put together a list of questions, some of which you should ask a prospective counsellor. You may already know the answers to some of the questions; pick out those that seem most relevant to you.

What are your qualifications? It is important that counsellors have qualifications as these ensure that a standard has been met, but qualifications are not everything and will not guarantee that they are a good counsellor.

Do you have supervision? This is important to know as all reputable counsellors must have regular supervision with a counsellor more experienced than themselves.

How much experience of counselling do you have? How many years have you been counselling? Experience can make a real difference, especially if the counsellor has experience in your issues. Those with less experience can still offer keenness and compassion.

How much do you charge, and how do you want this to be paid? Do you have a sliding scale? You need to know in advance how much or how little you will be charged and whether or not this is practical for you.

How many sessions do you offer? This can be linked to the previous question regarding affordability. Also, consider that some counsellors may state that there will be a minimum number of sessions and that a review will take place to check if further sessions are required or not.

What is your theoretical approach and way of working? You may resonate with one approach more than another, and it is vital to check out exactly what the approach involves and to feel comfortable with it. There is no consensus to state that one approach is any better than another. Some counsellors are experienced in more than one theoretical approach and will choose one to meet your specific needs.

Do you specialise in any issues? Many counsellors have additional qualifications in particular areas, and if you feel you would like a counsellor who specialises in your issues, then it is important to ensure a counsellor is able to help you with it.

Do you belong to any professional counselling bodies? In itself, belonging to a professional counselling body may mean very little. But it does suggest that the counsellor will be working with that body's code of ethics and may be reported to the professional body for any unprofessional conduct. Usually, a yearly fee will be paid by the counsellor, which indicates that they will be seen as working in a professional manner.

Are you accredited? An accredited counsellor is one who has achieved a recognised level of development, knowledge and experience. This is based upon an application to the professional body that they belong to, which includes completed documentation on training, supervision and practice.

How long is your waiting list? You may choose to wait until a counsellor has appointments to see you if you feel really comfortable with them or you may choose one with a short or no waiting list because you feel the need for help urgently. If the latter, then I would urge you to still go through the search procedure thoroughly and not opt for the counsellor out of urgency.

What happens if I miss or cancel a session? Some counsellors will still charge a fee or part of a fee if you miss a session without prior notice or miss a session giving less than twenty-four or forty-eight-hours prior notice. Similarly, if you cancel a session, a fee may have to be paid.

What is your confidentiality policy? All counsellors must have a confidentiality policy and are obliged to share this. It is imperative to know that what you share in the counselling sessions will remain confidential, with some exceptions that must be thoroughly explained to you. As part of confidentiality regarding your personal data, the General Data Protection Regulation must also be shared with you.

Have you ever had counselling? For me, this is a must-ask question because all counsellors in training should ideally have had some sessions of counselling as part of their training. It is difficult to imagine how anyone could be a counsellor who has never been a client. You do not need any details, but you need to know that the counsellor has also sat in the client's seat.

What do you expect from me? Whether or not you have had any counselling before, it is important to know what the counsellor requires from you. This may include regular attendance, motivation, authenticity and communicating your needs.

The right fit between you and the counsellor is imperative, a connection and a sense of trust being the most important aspects for a good counselling outcome. After asking the counsellor some of the above questions, ask yourself if the counsellor communicated with you in a way that made you feel comfortable, was it effective, and did it seem that you were compatible. you did not feel well matched, then you are not obliged to go ahead or to continue. Be cautious of those who show off and boast about their qualifications. Some counsellors delight in self-importance; it is intended to give a positive impression, but do not be taken in. Being pretentious is very often a sign of insecurity, and an insecure counsellor is the last person you want to share your issues with. Go with your instinct and trust your gut feeling.

Every counsellor is different, but difference is no indication that one is any better than another. To determine a good or bad counsellor, you do need to speak with them, preferably face to face, but on the phone is better than not speaking to them at all. This interaction will enable you to recognise any encouraging or warning signs. Almost all counsellors may be able to help you to make a tiny difference, but a good counsellor will help you to make an enormous difference. Always aim for a good counsellor; in certain organisations, you may not be given the choice. By asking the right questions, you may be able to avoid the bad ones. I offer the following lists to help you to appreciate the difference between good and bad counsellors.

Good counsellors should -

- Continue with their professional development, be a member of a professional counselling body and be regularly supervised.
- Be self-aware and know their limitations, and work within their theoretical approach appropriately.
- Work in an appropriate professional space, generate safety with no interruptions
- Offer and explain a counselling contract for working together and fully explain, jargon-free, their way of working.
- Maintain boundaries, such as time management and returning calls, emails, etc
- Develop a therapeutic relationship based on trust and rapport, and therapeutic distance.
- Be present and patient, empathic and caring, do not judge, and be caring, sensitive, responsible, warm, spontaneous and interested.

- Facilitate your understanding, growth and development, enabling you to manage your issues through support and challenge.

Aim to move you towards autonomy through encouragement and empowerment.

Ensure that you choose the best counsellor that you possibly can. Ask your questions and reputable counsellors will be only too happy to respond to them. Be sure that you feel comfortable with them and remain vigilant during any pre-session discussion and during that important first session.

Bad counsellors will –

- Not maintain boundaries, be late for sessions, cancel sessions, not return phone calls and not adhere to the session length.
- Be careful with your information, as they are less than efficient with confidentiality and sometimes refer to their other clients.
- Not be respectful, judge you and show a general lack of interest.
- Talk in psychological jargon, try to impress and talk about them-selves.
- Push you to share and disclose, something that you are not ready to and tell you what you should do.
- Tell you that you are their favourite client.
- Label you, insist that you continue with further counselling sessions.
- Make you feel judged, manipulated, or overly dependent.
- Pressure you into continuing therapy when you want to stop.

If you experience any of the above warning signs or you feel uncomfortable or vulnerable with the counsellor, then trust your inner feelings. If it were a pre-session discussion, then do not begin counselling, and if it was during the first or second session, then do not continue with the counselling. Counselling is a powerful process that requires the right kind of counsellor to engage with you. If one counsellor does not feel right, then look for another.

Below are two lists that may help with your choice of counsellor. They are in addition to what has already been offered. The first list reflects good counsellors, and the second list depicts some mediocre and bad counsellors

Consider a counsellor who –

- Is caring, sensitive, adaptable and flexible.
- Is discreet, open, self-aware and objective.
- Interested, encouraging and empowering.
- Challenges as well as supports, and who feels with you and not for you.
- Genuine and takes responsibility.
- Professional, ethical and humble
- Reliable, consistent and committed to their work.
- Regularly checks progress and believes in you.
- Has great awareness and can see beyond the spoken word.

Reject a counsellor who –

- Is disinterested, yawns, fidgets, clock watches, and does not make eye contact.
- Does not remember basic details and is dismissive of your issues.

- Is insensitive, makes you feel inferior, tells you what to do, talks too much.
- Initiates touch, is overly friendly, and makes you feel uncomfortable.
- Does not listen, constantly writes notes and continually asks, 'How you feel.
- Lacks expertise, ignores your feelings and gives advice.
- Tries to pressure you into continuing with counselling sessions and encourages dependency.
- Appears overwhelmed with your issues and is affected by your feelings.
- Avoids exploring emotions and does not ask permission before using various counselling techniques.

Diversity and Difference.

Not all counsellors have the same views on diversity and difference, whether it is race, colour, culture, sexual orientation, lifestyle, faith, ethnic or national origins. Every client must be treated fairly, equally and with respect. You should not tolerate any form of discrimination, and if you feel that your counsellor is being prejudicial then you must complain. Counsellors must ensure that they work with the principles of fairness and justice, and they must understand that differences can be visible or hidden. Assumptions about clients should never be made. Counsellors must understand how diversity and difference can affect clients. If counsellors lack cultural knowledge, then they should educate themselves about client groups through professional development. There is a great deal of variation between counsellors in relation to experience, understanding, support or acceptance. Never work with a counsellor who you feel is not accepting or is unsupportive, generally in relation to diversity issues.

Further Considerations.

Always remember that you can change counsellors if you feel any discomfort or if you believe that you are not getting what you need. You have every right to do this as a consumer receiving a service. If the service is not suitable for you as an individual or does not enable you to work with your issues, then do not continue. If you are able to discuss this with the counsellor face to face, then this is ideal, but if this is not possible, then phone them or the organisation to let them know or email/message the counsellor. The counsellor or organisation may or may not offer an alternative counsellor. Letting them know that you do not wish to continue and why may help the counsellor to appreciate that the way they work does not suit every individual client. Remember that you are the expert on you and that you have as much power in the therapeutic relationship as the counsellor.

Counselling is all about you, and you know all about yourself. The sessions are your sessions, and you are in control. You should expect and receive quality and competent counselling, delivered to the highest standards of knowledge and skill, by a counsellor who is committed, ethical, and honest. If your counsellor seems genuine and caring, if they accept you for who you are, if they value you and are actively working with you, then you, most likely, have a good counsellor. If you feel listened to and heard, if you feel a relationship is developing and if you feel safe to discuss your issues, your thoughts, and feelings then potentially this is a good match. If a counsellor is anything less than good, then they may be too eager to help or try to fix your problems for you, which may lead to overstepping boundaries. They may show their frustration or try to bamboozle you with 'counsellor speak.' More likely, they will have difficulty in empathising and may use a lot of pointless interventions and techniques to try to impress you to cover up their failings. You may be paying for your counselling, and you will certainly be dedicating your time and your energy to your counselling sessions, and as such, you have expectations of a positive outcome. Ensure that your counsellor is well-trained, experienced, professional and dependable. Counsellors are duty-bound to offer the best possible care to their clients. Unfortunately, a number of counsellors may fall short where knowledge and skills are concerned, they impair the purpose of counselling resulting in clients losing trust in the counsellor.

Personal Reflection.

Working with clients has been a huge privilege and extraordinarily humbling. *I have had the opportunity to work with many individuals from all walks of life, with numerous issues. It is the rapport and therapeutic relationship, when developed between counsellor and client, that forms a foundation of trust, which is important for the counselling process. I have been aware of many people who have had unpleasant experiences in unproductive counselling. Experiences like these should never happen; they can cause mental and emotional upset and great distress.*

I remember so many of the clients I have counselled, some for shorter periods, others for longer. All worked really hard, and over time, they all made positive changes. It was a moving and often humbling experience to accompany these clients throughout their counselling.

You deserve the very best counsellors and counselling, and I urge you to not to accept anything less. Counsellors must be respectful to everyone and must be aware of disabilities, gender identities, difference and, diversity and neurodiversity. Search for a counsellor who is a good fit as it can make a huge difference. It is important to feel comfortable and safe, and always trust your instincts. Asking the counsellor questions will help you to understand what counselling is all about. Check prospective counsellor qualifications and look for accredited professionals. Consider counsellors' specialisms such as trauma, relationships, and anxiety, for example. Think about whether you want face- to-face or remote counselling, also reflect on the cost and availability. Be aware of unregulated counsellors, hidden costs, those who guarantee quick results and newly qualified counsellors. Speak to counsellors before booking sessions, ask questions, check how comfortable you feel talking to them and whether you think they may be a good fit or not.

Chapter Four

The Nuts And Bolts Of The Fifty Minute Hour

A Closer Look at the Therapeutic Encounter

'Each session is a quiet connection, encompassing skill, intuition and empathy.'

Seeking support is rarely straight forward; this chapter will help you to navigate the counselling journey. Many things happen in counselling sessions, some of which you may be aware of, and a substantial amount of which you probably are not. It is important that you, as a client, understand what the counselling process entails, as this can help to alleviate any preconceptions, concerns, or anxiety. Knowing what counselling involves and what to expect will enable you to appreciate how it may benefit you. I will provide a considerable amount of information to help you to understand what counselling entails, along with clarification on aspects that may answer some of the questions you have. Gaining insight into the counselling process can have a meaningful effect on your experience, especially during the first few sessions.

Counselling can feel daunting for many people, especially if you are concerned about what to expect. You may initially feel confused or hesitant, and that is completely normal. I will share what should and should not happen as you begin your counselling. It is only natural to wonder what you are entering into when you book a series of counselling sessions. The most important things to remember are that counsellors should not have expectations of their clients. They should remain unbiased, avoid judgment, and offer feedback that is objective and constructive. While no two counsellors work in exactly the same way, all should follow the professional code of ethics and conduct themselves with integrity.

Personal Reflection.

My very first experience of counselling took place in the early days of this talking therapy. *When I entered the counselling room, there were no explanations given to me, no contracts, and no clarification. At the time, I did not know exactly what counselling was or what the counsellor would expect of me. I did not know what happens in a session, or even who a counsellor was. I had no idea how long the session would last or how many sessions I would have. I had no real sense of what was going to transpire. I had no choice in who my counsellor would be, and I was concerned about who else might be informed about my issues.*

Numerous clients today still feel confused and distressed when they are not given sufficient information about counselling. Counselling should never be like this, which is one of the reasons I wrote this book. Clients must be well informed about all aspects of counselling and should never feel bewildered, confused, or uneasy before, during, or after the process. Counsellors should always make time to offer clients clear information and should never leave them anxious and uncertain at a stage when they most need reassurance and compassion.

What issues can you take to counselling?

The list below is not, by any means, an exhaustive one, but it offers some of the main issues that counsellors can help with.

- Stress, anxiety, low moods, depression.
- Bereavement, grief, isolation, loneliness, helplessness.
- Separation, divorce, relationship difficulties.
- Self-harm, eating disorders, bullying.

- ➢ Anger management, addictions (e.g. alcohol, drugs, gambling).
- ➢ Trauma, abuse, redundancy, domestic violence.
- ➢ Anger, bullying, health anxiety, phobias.
- ➢ Past events from childhood or adulthood, current life events.
- ➢ Obsessions and compulsions, pregnancy, miscarriage.
- ➢ Work, career issues plus many more.

What exactly happens in Counselling?

Counselling is what is called a talking therapy, and this is because what happens in the sessions is a discourse between a counsellor and a client. This will be very different from talking to a friend or relative. It should take place in a safe space, so that there will be no psychological or physical harm to you, and, importantly, it must be confidential. Confidentiality allows you to share whatever you wish, which will never be repeated by the counsellor or misused. It is the counsellor's duty to protect your details and maintain your privacy and ensure that whatever you discuss will remain in the counselling room, with some exemptions. Although counsellors are bound by confidentiality, there are certain situations when breaching confidentiality is necessary, such as ethical, safety or legal concerns. Some examples are court orders, criminal activity, risk of harm and child protection. If there is a need to breach confidentiality, then the counsellor will discuss this with you initially and assess the risk. For the counsellor, breaching confidentiality has to be very carefully considered.

All the focus of the session should be on you, the client. It is essential that you meet with the counsellor regularly at the same time and on the same day, usually weekly, but this may vary. Your counsellor is there to help you to work with your issue(s) by enabling you to understand yourself and your experiences. It is important to feel relaxed with the counsellor, and once they have invited you to discuss your issue(s) they should listen and offer you their full attention. The counsellor should not offer their viewpoints or opinions or criticise you in any way. They should not offer advice or their own beliefs. What they should do is to show empathy and ask questions for clarification and further understanding. If you are quiet and thoughtful, then they should manage this silence.

The counsellor should be encouraging and empowering to help you to achieve your objectives. You lead the sessions, and the counsellor will be guided by you. You will not be pressured into talking about anything you feel uncomfortable with. What you choose to talk about is entirely up to you. The counsellor should initially enable the development of a relationship. The relationship is a therapeutic one, which means it is based upon professional intimacy, which encompasses caring, trust, respect, and honesty. Counselling allows you to share your issues and the feelings that are affecting you emotionally. They should enable you to consider changes that will result in your emotional well-being. Counselling can be life-changing for many. It can help you to understand yourself better, make sense of your past and present. It is a place where empathy is offered, and counsellors will never push you to talk about anything that may feel uncomfortable.

The way a counsellor works will depend on the theoretical approach they use. The approaches are all different, but each one has the same aim: to help you. As an example, the counsellor may invite you to engage in more creative ways of working that are appropriate for you and your issue(s). These are generally for you to consider between sessions.

Creative ways of working may include drawing, writing, the use of your own photographs or of your favourite music. The counsellor may give you diagrams to illustrate relationships and connections or useful written information for you to read between sessions, and even breathing and relaxation techniques. You can then bring your thoughts and anything that you may have written or drawn to the next session, including music or photographs. These methods will often generate increased discussion, enable expression or self-understanding by encouraging you to connect more with your thoughts and feelings. They may help to develop innovative ideas and perspectives. Creative ways of working are not for everyone, but they can be useful for clients who may be struggling to express themselves or to explain their thoughts and emotions. They can be especially useful for children and young people, as well as many adults. The counsellor must introduce creative techniques with an initial discussion, and you do not have to partake in creative ways of working if you do not feel comfortable with them. They should be explained by the counsellor, and then you should be given the option of trying them or not. The use of creative therapeutic approaches in counselling can help clients to access their visual, auditory and experiential ways of communicating.

Personal Reflection.

I have used creative methods when working with various clients, often with beneficial results. *I always ensured that clients understood why I was offering a creative approach and clarified that it was appropriate for their needs. It is not suitable for a counsellor to use creative techniques in every session, especially without adequate* *explanation. I have encountered a few counsellors who have used creative methods in unethical ways, as well as some inexperienced practitioners who rely on them because they struggle to maintain the counselling approaches.*

When creative techniques are used inappropriately, they can have harmful effects on clients. If the counsellor does not explain the approach clearly, then clients are left confused. I have supervised counsellors who overuse creative methods or do not fully appreciate the techniques they are applying. These counsellors may, unfortunately, leave clients feeling overwhelmed and distressed.

Counsellors work in many different ways with clients, depending on the theoretical approach that they use. There are many methods involved in theoretical approaches. Each approach will use different methods, but they will all be aimed at helping you. The methods are tailored to your specific needs to support your progress and development. When they are used efficiently, they can help you to view yourself and your issue(s) differently.

Myths about Counselling.

There are many myths about counselling, some of which can be off-putting. The following myths may enable you to gain a better understanding of counselling. It is important to appreciate that counselling, when it is presented on television, may offer one or two aspects that are genuinely used in counselling, but in reality, most of what is offered it is very different.

Counselling is weird and magic. The more you are informed about counsellors and counselling, the less weird it appears. There is no mystique, the counsellor does not wave a magic wand, and issues will not disappear by chanting a few special words.

Counselling is a quick fix. Depending upon the client, the issues, the counsellor, and the therapeutic approach used, the counselling will take as short or as long as is necessary. My experience would suggest that, for a small number of clients, as few as four sessions can be sufficient and, for other clients, the sessions may extend to many more. It is not a quick fix for anyone or for any issue.

Counselling will help all people and all issues. Not all people will benefit from counselling, and not all issues can be alleviated by counselling. This is often because the counsellor may not be adequately experienced or may not be sufficiently knowledgeable in helping with certain client issues.

Counsellors can read minds. Good counsellors can often read between your words and appreciate what you are not saying as much as what you are saying, but no mind-reading is involved.

Counselling is for weak people. This could not be further from the truth. To take the first step towards counselling is courageous. Anyone who undertakes counselling shows strength and resilience.

Counsellors tell you what to do and give advice. Counsellors do not tell you what to do or how to live your life; they do not make decisions for you or recommend a course of action. Counsellors enable and empower you to make your own decisions. They should support you in whatever you decide to do in your life.

Counsellors just listen and say nothing. If this is the case, then you need to change your counsellor immediately. It would be natural to expect that you, the client, will be talking more than the counsellor, but certainly the counsellor should be responding at regular times, explaining, clarifying, supporting and gently challenging.

Counsellors will fix me. Counsellors do not fix people; they facilitate you, the client, to heal yourself.

Assessment Session.

As briefly outlined in the previous chapter, it is usual to have an assessment session or pre-counselling meeting prior to beginning your counselling journey. This will vary tremendously depending upon whether you are using a private counsellor, a voluntary counselling organisation, an employee-assisted programme or through the National Health Service. Counsellors and organisations who do offer assessment sessions may invite you for a face-to -face session or it may take place over the phone, on a video chat, or a counselling pack may be sent by post or email. This pack will contain information and forms for you to complete, which, in most cases, need to be posted or emailed back to the counsellor or organisation, or they may be brought into the first counselling session. The assessment session usually lasts for up to thirty minutes, longer for some counsellors, and it may or may not be the counsellor that you will be seeing regularly, who takes the assessment session.

Not all organisations or counsellors will offer this assessment session. In this case, all the administration, questions and discussions that usually occur in the assessment or pre-counselling session will be completed in the first session of counselling. The assessment session offers an opportunity for you to be introduced to the counsellor and for you to have your questions answered. Essential information can be explained to you, such as confidentiality and the General Data Protection Regulation, which outlines how your information will be used and stored and your rights as a client. Counselling supervision should be explained, and when counselling reviews will take place. The counselling contract will also be given to you and explained, and if you wish to continue, then you will be asked to sign the contract, and a copy will be given to you to keep. You will complete a form with your details, such as contact number, email, any medication that you take and the name of your general practitioner. You will be asked about your reasons for requesting counselling and what you hope to gain from counselling. The assessment sessions vary between individual counsellors and organisations.

Some counsellors and organisations may also use measurement tools, which are forms with lists of questions for you to answer. The most popular ones are general anxiety disorder, clinical outcomes in routine evaluation and patient health questionnaire. They have been designed to reflect how you are feeling. Such forms may be used periodically throughout the counselling or may be given at the beginning and end of counselling. General anxiety disorder looks for the presence of any anxiety and asks seven questions scored from zero to three, the scores being added to assess levels of anxiety. Clinical outcomes in routine evaluation have ten questions, scored zero to four, which assess several issues, of which some are depression, anxiety and general functioning. Patient Health Questionnaires screen for depression with nine questions, scored from zero to four.

The reasons the counsellors use these questionnaires is to gauge an outline of how a client is feeling, and they can help to inform the counsellor in terms of how to progress and what approach to take. When these questionnaires are used throughout the counselling sessions, then counsellors can see the progress being made through the scores. The scores may also indicate any deterioration or if a client needs urgent support. Whilst these measurement tools may be useful, I am not especially a fan of them. They can take up precious time and be annoying for clients when used continually. The time would be better spent reassuring and getting to know the client, and enabling them to understand the contract and the boundaries of the relationship. Using them throughout the counselling sessions wastes time. For some clients, the use of these measurement tools may help the counsellor, but if they are used, then they should be sparingly. Some counsellors, including myself, would rather have a discussion about how clients are feeling in terms of anxiety, depression, and generally coping.

A counselling contract must always be in writing and signed by both parties. A verbal contract, unless the counsellor records it, is worthless, and my advice would be not to continue the counselling unless a signed and dated written contract is completed. The contract should be very clear, concise and written in jargon-free language. The document is an opportunity for the counsellor to state what they are offering to you. It should be discussed with you and an opportunity offered for you to ask questions before you sign it.

It should make you feel more comfortable about the entire process of counselling. Also, it should assure you that the counselling will take place in a safe environment, that it will be confidential and conducted in a professional manner. The responsibilities of both counsellor and client should be emphasised. There must always be flexibility in a counselling contract regarding certain aspects. It may need to be changed, or something added (if a signal is lost or the sound is not clear, etc.); issues that may be connected to alcohol or drug dependency (if a client may be under the influence during the counselling session, etc.); clients with disabilities (if aids or other needs are required). The contract, once signed, will indicate your informed consent. If the counselling is for a young person or for a vulnerable adult, then it may be necessary to request written consent from a parent or guardian.

***I have included extracts of most of the documents referred to here in chapter* 5.**

Number of sessions.

Counselling involves a series of planned, regular sessions; the actual number of sessions will be discussed at the beginning of counselling. In some cases, several sessions may be offered and reviewed when these sessions end to determine whether further sessions are required. Some counselling is open-ended, which means that there is no limit to how many sessions are offered. When considering the number of sessions required, it is difficult for me to estimate due to different counsellor approaches, ways of working, differing client needs and client issues. However, as a very rough guide, around six sessions would be a minimum, twenty plus would constitute longer term, and the average will often be ten to fifteen sessions. Normally, counselling sessions are weekly, but there are variations in certain circumstances for example, fortnightly when nearing the end of counselling or for financial reasons, also, twice a week for a brief period of time in extenuating circumstances. Counsellors state that sessions last for an hour, but this again varies as, more recently, the counselling hour has become fifty minutes. Be prepared for a counselling hour to last for fifty minutes or sixty minutes. For children and young people, it may be thirty to forty minutes. Once established, it should be consistent throughout the whole series of sessions. In the first counselling session, you may feel anxious, a little less so if you had an assessment session with your counsellor. Feeling anxious is a normal reaction which should get easier as the sessions progress. As counselling takes time and effort from yourself, it cannot be rushed, and a few sessions will not offer a quick fix. Conversely, having endless sessions is also not ideal, as dependence may develop.

Review Sessions.

Periodically, during your counselling, a counsellor may conduct a review session. Monitoring and evaluating the counselling is essential throughout all the counselling sessions and is an important part of counselling. The number of reviews will be dependent upon the number of sessions undertaken. On average, a review may be used every six sessions, but can be applied at any time during the counselling if it feels helpful or appropriate. The counsellor should always let you know during the previous session that there will be a review in the following session. The review is always verbal, and it is a collaborative experience which should reflect on all the counselling sessions. It aims to check on client progress, the client-counsellor relationship and the theoretical approach being used. It is also useful for clients to consider whether their needs are being met, to decide what they would like from future sessions or what may be most useful to focus on currently. It is important to note that reviews are not evaluating clients but rather the counselling work and the best ways to move forward. Reviews are also used at the end of a course of counselling to strengthen and support a client's future plans and to assess what has been accomplished.

Individual Counselling Sessions.

Each individual counselling session will be different, but all will have a beginning, middle and end. Many beginning sessions follow on from the previous session, but this is dependent upon you and what you choose to discuss in the session and how you are feeling at the time. Some counsellors will briefly recap the main issues from the previous session, whilst others will check out how you are and what may have happened since the last session or simply ask what you would like to discuss or work on in the current session. Following on from the beginning of the session will be the middle part of the session, where time will be given for you to reflect on thoughts, feelings, actions, past experiences and present challenges. Normally, you will continue to work on the main issue or move onto underlying issues, which may take over the session. Silence may arise in some sessions, which will be part of the process. Silences are for you to think about something that you may have said, or the counsellor may say something for you to consider. The counsellor will be giving you some space for this, but will not allow the silence to go on for too long. It should feel natural rather than awkward.

Towards the end of the session, usually within five or ten minutes before the end of the session, the counsellor should indicate to you that the session will close shortly. They should gently and safely close down the issue being discussed, briefly summarise the main aspects from the session and add anything positive that may be helpful. They should further ensure that you are emotionally comfortable to end the session and confirm the next appointment.

At the end of each individual counselling session, it may be useful to give yourself some time, if possible, to wind down. Perhaps having a walk or sitting quietly at home or meeting a friend in a cafe for a drink. Depending on how the counselling session has left you feeling, choose something that either allows you to feel good or something to let go of sadness or low spirits.

Timing and Notes

Timing is very important and is the responsibility of the counsellor. Sessions must begin on time and end on time. Time must be utilised effectively during each session. Prior to each session, counsellors should read the notes from the previous session and at the end of each session, they should make notes on the main points of the current session. These are called session notes; they may also make notes for their supervision, which are called process notes. Process notes are written to be used in the counsellor's supervision sessions. They focus more on the counselling and the counsellor's process. They are confidential with no client details contained within them. These notes enable the counsellor to discuss issues related to themselves, their counselling and aspects of their client work with their supervisor, to ensure effective counselling practice.

Session notes are used as an aid for memory and should be a requirement for all counsellors. They may help if ever a complaint was made by a client or if legal action occurred. As part of the General Data Protection Regulations, clients may request to see their session notes at any time. These notes should be fairly brief, and details of the session need to be concise. Counsellor's opinions should not be included. Client notes are confidential, with the exceptions of clients requesting to see them or for legal action. They should be stored securely and separately from client information. They are normally kept for several years from the end of the counselling, and then they can be suitably destroyed. Notes kept electronically need to be password-protected and also should be encrypted.

Preparing for the first session.

In order to get the very best from counselling, consider making a list of questions that you may want to ask the counsellor and ensure that you know the issue(s) that you would like the counsellor to help you with. It is really useful to reflect on these. Try to relax and manage any stress as best you can. Plan your journey if the counselling is face-to-face and arrive a few minutes early. For video or phone counselling, ensure that you are in a comfortable and private room. Consider your goals, what you may want to achieve from counselling and focus on your own experience. Try to be open- minded and trust yourself. Be prepared for preliminaries and questions from the counsellor. Above all ensure that you are able to feel comfortable with the counsellor. It may be useful for you to assess the counsellor during the session to make sure that you feel relaxed and that you have confidence in and are able to trust them. This, in turn, will enable a working relationship to develop. Be consistent in attending sessions as this will help to build progress. Getting upset or distressed in sessions is normal, and counsellors understand this and can help you to overcome this. be open and honest, share your thoughts and feelings.

What to expect from the first session.

The first session will establish the groundwork. You will be welcomed, and introductions will be made. The counsellor should explain all about themselves, the counselling and such things as confidentiality and boundaries. If all the documentation has been completed, then the counsellor will address your issue(s) and ask questions to understand your needs. They will discuss what you want to gain from counselling and the focus of the session. Everything should be made clear to you, and you should begin to feel trust developing. Ask all your questions which the counsellor should answer. Discuss what is on your mind at your own pace. Communicate openly and honestly. The first few sessions may feel a little awkward. Many prospective clients feel nervous before and during their first session, and this is normal. The counsellor will create a safe space for you to share your issue(s) at your own pace. You may feel emotional or challenged; all these feelings are valid. Counselling is your safe and confidential space. Be prepared to experience strong feelings or have unexpected reactions; these are all normal.

Between Sessions.

The time between counselling sessions gives you an opportunity to self-reflect, consider and process all that was worked with in the previous session, and to assess your emotions. Often, good progress can be made between sessions. Thinking about what was discussed, implementing strategies for coping with stress and anxiety, reassuring yourself and positive thinking. You may decide to start writing a journal or list what you would like to discuss or questions to ask the counsellor in your next session. Some counsellors may offer informative leaflets or documents for you to read, which may help you to understand aspects of yourself or your issue(s) further. Not all counsellors, but some counsellors may give you what we loosely term 'homework'. 'Homework' may be writing a journal, your thoughts and feelings, or making a note of when you feel at your worst or what triggers certain feelings. You may be given forms to record your thoughts or to monitor your moods. Other counsellors may encourage you to prepare something related to your issue(s) for the next counselling session, for example, something that you enjoy doing, such as creating a poem, or a drawing/painting, a book or a story to discuss. This creative process will allow you to think, evaluate and consider, it may help to produce a greater sense of yourself.

If you start to feel confused or overwhelmed, then let your counsellor know and try breathing exercises and daily walks. If you feel that it is all too much to bear, then ask for help from a friend, a member of your family or contact your general practitioner. You can dial nine- one- one, or National Health Service one-one-one or contact a crisis line, for example, Mind or the Samaritans. Knowing what to expect and what is likely to happen in counselling can be extremely helpful for you to make the decision as to whether counselling is for you or not. Understanding how counselling works and what happens in the sessions is paramount. Sitting in front of a stranger and sharing personal and private concerns can feel unsettling, a little like embarking on a journey into the unknown. However, knowing what to expect will make it feel less daunting. Counsellors are there to help you with your issues.

Remote counselling.

For me, there is nothing better than face-to-face counselling; the physical presence of a client and a counsellor can enable the development of the working relationship in counselling, where a connection is made, which can support and facilitate the counselling work. However, with the increase in the use of technology, remote counselling has begun to be accepted as a viable alternative to face-to-face counselling. It does have its limitations, but for more and more people, it is a relevant alternative to face-to-face counselling. Remote counselling can be telephone conversations, messaging, email or video. Remote counselling can be more affordable; it is also beneficial for anyone living in a remote area. People with physical limitations would benefit from remote counselling, such as disabled, housebound, mobility issues or even agoraphobia. There are also people who prefer anonymity. It may also be a more useful way of working for the younger generation. It is really important for you to ascertain that, when working remotely, the counsellor is qualified, experienced, has a good understanding of the technology used and has undergone training in remote counselling. Be certain that the online counsellor is who they actually say they are.

There are pros and cons to remote counselling that need to be considered. Some of the disadvantages are technology issues, for instance, if the internet connection is lost. The main one, for me, would be confidentiality and privacy with all forms of remote counselling. For the counsellor, there is no way to consider a client's body language unless it is video counselling. Some clients may have difficulty in putting their thoughts and feelings into written words for messaging and email counselling. Body language offers a great deal of information and enables a counsellor to get a clear picture of a client's feelings, thoughts and behaviour, such as non-verbal cues, facial expressions and even tone of voice. Some of the advantages of remote counselling are accessibility, flexibility and convenience, especially for those who work shifts or irregular hours.

Stages of the counselling process.

The whole process of counselling is divided into three distinct stages: the beginning, the middle and the ending. Within each individual session, there will also be a beginning, middle and ending. Each counselling session should be tailored to suit you individually and the specific issue(s) you are bringing. The process throughout all sessions should be well structured, and the counsellor should enable it to be a positive experience for you. The counsellor should always be reviewing the process and the progress being made, and should be using their skills to hold you. Holding is a term used symbolically and not literally; it refers to emotional holding in that the counsellor is there for you, being perceptive, recognising and accepting your feelings.

The room where your counselling takes place is important, especially in terms of it being a confidential space with no distractions such as photographs or ornaments. It should feel safe and comfortable. The chairs for you and the counsellor must be comfortable and should not be too close or too distant, and not directly facing each other. There must be no barrier between the seating, like a desk or coffee table. Ideally, the lighting in the room should be soft, windows should have blinds, noise from outside must be minimal, and no one outside of the room should be able to hear what is being said inside the room.

Beginning Sessions.

Part of the first session, if this has not been done previously, will be to collect your information and discuss the contract and boundaries. Confidentiality will be explained as well as supervision, and the counsellor will ask about your issue(s) and your goals. This is a good time for you to ask the counsellor any questions that you may have.

Assuming that all the administration has been completed, there will be introductions and rapport building. One of the most important aspects of the beginning stage is the development of a therapeutic relationship. This relationship, between you and the counsellor, must be based on trust by both parties. It has to be judgment-free; you must feel comfortable and able to communicate and engage with each other. The counsellor should be listening to you, and you must feel heard as you share your issue(s). Sharing and engaging in the counselling will enable the therapeutic relationship to develop, and it must be present in order for the counselling work to move forward. For this first session, I would encourage you to consider how you feel about the counsellor and counselling. If you are uncomfortable or anxious in any way, then consider talking about this with the counsellor, and if there is no improvement, then you must end the counselling and find another counsellor. Your counsellor will ask you questions for clarification on certain aspects so that they can understand your situation and determine the focus and priority of the work. Throughout these sessions, the counsellor will be gathering information and considering you and your issues(s) to best determine your needs and the most efficient way to work with you. The counsellor will be encouraging you to share your thoughts and concerns and to identify your emotions. You should feel valued and understood by the counsellor who must give you their full attention to you and show genuine interest.

Middle Sessions.

The middle sessions commence after the beginning sessions end, when your issues have been aired and discussed, and the therapeutic relationship has been established. By this time the counsellor will have a general understanding of you and your concerns. The middle sessions form the main section of the work and last longer than the beginning and ending sessions. The counselling relationship should deepen, and there should be a good rapport. The counselling work will become more intense, and exploration will go deeper. Emotions will be processed, and progress will be reviewed. The counsellor will use therapeutic techniques to encourage you to identify and integrate your thoughts and feelings. This will help you to gain insight into your issue(s). The counsellor will be identifying patterns, triggers and underlying concerns to enable you to obtain more of a perspective.

Towards the end of these middle sessions, there should be progress towards preparation for moving towards achieving what you hoped to gain from counselling. Interventions from the counsellor should assist in enabling this progress and linking it to appropriate actions. This, in turn, should encourage change, growth and development that ultimately help you to move towards achieving your desired outcomes. In some cases, further counselling sessions may be required for additional intensive counselling.

Ending Sessions.

The final sessions of the counselling will consider your achievements. These sessions are extremely important in terms of moving towards a mutually agreed, well-timed and effective ending. Ending counselling, having accomplished what you wanted, can be a fulfilling experience. For some clients it may be emotional or even difficult, and the counsellor must be aware of this and encourage clients to reflect on the counselling sessions and on the future. You must feel that progress has been made, that you feel comfortable about the sessions finishing and also about accepting the conclusion of the counselling relationship. It is important for you to ensure that the time for ending is right for you. The counsellor should never abruptly terminate counselling, and there should be adequate preparation for it. The counsellor must assess your readiness for ending and discuss this with you, relevant coping strategies, any concerns, doubts and misconceptions that you may have, which should be thoroughly considered and talked through. In some instances, counsellors may suggest a follow-up session or that further counselling will be available in the future if required. A date for the end will be jointly arranged so that you can prepare yourself for it.

During the final session, there should be a review of the counselling and your experience of it in terms of where you were at the beginning and where you are at the end. There should be general reflection and recognition of the counselling relationship ending on a positive note. Your safety for ending is paramount and should include your willingness for ending, the support you may have in place, your thoughts and feelings about ending, changes you have made and considerations for the future, plus new awareness and understanding.

It is normal to have a mixture of thoughts and emotions about finishing counselling. It will be dependent on the experience that you have had and the relationship you have formed with the counsellor. There is no one particular way you are supposed to feel.

Counselling is about growth and healing. Awareness and courage are needed when ending counselling, which should be empowering, where you can walk away with hope and strength.

If you are worried about how you will cope, then share with the counsellor how you are feeling. They might be able to help you to plan things that you can do after counselling has ended to help you to work out your next steps. The beginning builds trust, the middle works through issues, and the ending consolidates progress.

Chapter Five

Documents, Supporting Information And Records

Standards and compliance

'Essential information, files, facts and paper trails'

In the last decade or so, the amount of paperwork and documentation in all professions has increased enormously, and counselling is no exception. Counselling has evolved significantly over the years, and the increase in paperwork is due to a variety of reasons such as personal and professional accountability, demonstrating effectiveness, legal and ethical practice and transparency. All the paperwork is of benefit to both counsellors and clients. I do, however, appreciate that, for clients, the documentation can feel an inconvenience; even so, much of this documentation is necessary and very helpful.

Counsellors will work with many documents for all different circumstances, but I am focusing on the documentation that affects you as a client. I offer some partial examples of the forms, most of which you may be asked to complete. All the forms used in counselling are adaptable and will be different for each individual counsellor or counselling organisation. Some may be brief and others quite lengthy. A number may be easy to understand and complete, whilst the remainder may be a little more difficult to comprehend and answer.

The forms I offer below are not complete; they are purely brief examples of what you may expect. Many counsellors and counselling organisations offer prospective clients an information document about counselling. These can be extremely helpful as they will guide you through what counselling is all about. I offer a brief example below.

Introduction to counselling information sheet.

Counselling is a talking therapy where trained and qualified counsellors work with clients over a period of time to enable them to share their issues and to gain insight and awareness. There are many different ways of working in counselling, and, as such, the counsellor will explain to you their way of working. The counsellor will offer a safe and confidential space for you to share your concerns, thoughts and feelings.

The counsellor will help you to find your own solutions, enable you to make changes and listen to you without any judgement. Counselling may include talking about the past and the present, about relationships, your feelings and emotions.

Counselling can take place face to face, by telephone or online. Seeking counselling is an important and positive step towards your well-being.

Counselling is confidential; whatever you discuss in counselling sessions will be in confidence, and your counsellor will not talk about you or your issues with anyone else. The exception will be in certain circumstances that your counsellor will discuss with you in your initial meeting.

A contract will be explained to you together with the boundaries of the counselling relationship. You are free to ask any questions that you wish prior to beginning counselling.

Some counsellors and organisations may send a welcome pack to you which contains lots of information such as costs, length of sessions, your rights as a client and much more. These can be very helpful, but not all counsellors use them. They can offer a lot of useful details and even some of the forms for you to complete, a welcome letter, practice policies and pre-session preparation.

Moving on to the forms that you will be asked to complete. The first form is the client information sheet that requires your basic details. Below is an example of what you may be asked to complete on this form. The amount of information requested may vary. On some forms, you may be asked for more details such as employment status, family history, and marital status.

This form may also be used jointly with a client assessment form.

Client information / intake form.

Date: Full name: Date of birth: Address: Phone number: Email address: Emergency contact:

Relationship to client:(where applicable) Health issues: Medications: G.P. name and contact details:

This client assessment form, which may be combined with the client information form, will be completed by an assessor or the counsellor themselves, depending on where the counselling is accessed. The form will be completed by asking you questions. It is used to gain information about you so as to appreciate your needs, issues and goals and your reasons for embarking on counselling. The counsellor can then use this information to assess how to move forward and to meet your needs. The questions asked are just the beginning of your counselling journey.

Again, each individual counsellor's form will be different and other questions may be asked, such as alcohol intake, substance use and what support you have. All the questions help to begin building rapport and to enable the counsellor to understand more about you and your issues, and this will introduce the start of the therapeutic relationship.

Client Assessment Form.

What are your issues? How long have you had these issues for? How are you coping?

Have you had counselling before? What do you hope to gain from counselling?

What have you done to help with the issues? Any self-harm or suicidal ideation:

Any other relevant information:

Privacy and consent relate to the General Data Protection Regulation and the use of your personal data by the counsellor or counselling organisation. Personal data includes, for example, your name, phone number, email address, date of birth, gender and home address. Your data will be collected and safely stored. This form may be introduced to you during the initial assessment session. It should be

explained to you in detail, and any questions that you have should be answered. You will be asked to sign this form to give your consent and your permission for the counsellor or counselling organisation to process your data. Collecting and processing your data is a contractual obligation for counsellors. The information that you give will enable the counsellor to determine whether or not counselling can be offered. Every privacy and consent form will be different; some may be concise, others very lengthy. The example below should indicate briefly what you may expect from this form.

Privacy and consent form.

You will be asked to sign this form during the assessment session, giving your informed consent for processing your data. General Data Protection Regulation Act 2018 and Privacy

Electronic Communications 2003.

Your information will be used to provide you with a professional counselling service, to offer suitable appointments with a counsellor.

To notify you of any appointment changes and to offer you an opportunity to give feedback.

Your information is stored securely, and all electronic records are password-protected. We will answer any questions that you may have on any of the issues in this form.

As a client, you have certain rights in relation to your data.

To Be Informed: The right to know how the data is collected, processed and used.

Right of Access: The right to request access to your personal data.

I have read the Privacy and Consent form, and I give my consent for X Counselling Organisation to process my data. Date: Signature:

The Counselling Contract is an essential document with a lot of information. It may be offered at the initial assessment session. It is an important form that needs to be read and signed. The counsellor or assessor should explain the details to you and answer all of your questions. Counselling contracts will vary; in the main, they should contain similar significant details. Some counselling documents will differ slightly depending upon whether the counselling is face-to-face, telephone counselling or video counselling. This contract is a formal agreement between the counsellor and the client. It forms the terms and details of the counselling relationship. It outlines the relationship and working alliance, the responsibilities and rights of the counsellor and client. It encompasses safety and professionalism, the responsibilities of client and counsellor, it sets expectations and defines the boundaries. The contract will also cover confidentiality.

Successful counselling is very much dependent upon the development of a therapeutic relationship, and a good therapeutic relationship relies on the working agreement establishing the context for the counselling work. A counsellor who is professional and respectful, offering a safe space, who answers your questions and who clearly explains the agreement is essential. Some of what should be included in the contract are confidentiality, counsellor's supervision sessions, complaints, costs, time and place, amongst several other important aspects.

The counsellor should discuss the contact with you, ideally at the assessment session.

Counselling contracts should include the following, although this is not a comprehensive list.

Counselling Contract.

The counsellor is a member of the British Association for Counselling and Psychotherapy and works within their Ethical Framework.

Counsellor's name and Qualifications

This document is a mutual agreement between the counsellor and the client, which will be discussed and signed before counselling commences. It sets out the responsibilities of the client and the counsellor.

Fees for each session Payable to…

Cancellation and non-attendance of sessions, e.g. twenty-four or forty-eight hours' notice, then re-arranged at no extra charge, or no notice given a fee is payable.

Complaints procedure – please see the separate document.

Confidentiality – A really important aspect of counselling where everything discussed in each counselling session is kept in the strictest confidence.

The counsellor receives regular supervision where your name will never be disclosed.

The counsellor will keep brief notes of each counselling session.

Sessions – 50 minutes in duration on a weekly basis at the same time and place. A minimum of six sessions will be offered with a view to extending if required.

Early termination will be allowed under special circumstances.

Out-of-session contact is not allowed. Counsellors' way of working is...

Signed: Date: Counsellor:

Signed: Date: Client:

There may be several other aspects of the various counsellors' contracts. The above document forms a general example only. Additions to the above will be for contracts other than face-to-face, such as telephone or video counselling, where it is essential to include important information related to these different forms of counselling. These additions are for anything that may not run smoothly in the sessions, mainly technical problems. For example, a phone session is cut off, the phone call becomes inaudible or the client does not answer the phone call. Another example would be for online counselling, where, for example, there are difficulties with the internet or the sound is missing one way or the other.

Online/Telephone Counselling

As above, plus the following (example only) –

We will meet through secure Zoom (for example)

OR We will meet via telephone.

This will be on a weekly basis at the same time on the same day for fifty minutes.

I will always make contact with you at the beginning of each session.

I will offer total privacy, and I require that you have total privacy in a quiet location.

If you are late, I will not be able to lengthen the session.

If there are technical problems before (connection issues) or during the session (audio-related, poor visuals, freezing, etc.) then we can reschedule the session. I will send you a text message or email to arrange this.

The Complaint Form.

You can choose to complete a complaint form if you are receiving counselling from an

organisation or if you are seeing a counsellor privately and that counsellor is a member of a professional body. You also have a choice as to how you make your complaint, which may be by letter, email, phone or in person. The actual complaints procedure should be offered on the form, but procedures will vary within each organisation and also between private counsellors. Usually, it will take the format of initially speaking with the counsellor to try to resolve the issue. If this is not comfortable for you, then you may follow the internal complaints procedure or finally make a formal complaint.

Making a complaint is not an easy thing to do, but if you feel that you have been treated unfairly, inappropriately or judgmentally, or that your counsellor has been unethical,

incompetent or disinterested, or if you feel uncomfortable in any way, then you must complain. The partial example below for a Complaints Form is to merely offer you an idea of what to expect. The procedure of dealing with your complaint should also be evident on the form.

Complaints Form and Procedure.

If you feel that you would like to make a complaint because you are dissatisfied with the service that you have received, please complete this form in as much detail as possible so that we can resolve the situation as quickly for you.

Be assured that all complaints are handled with the utmost confidentiality.

Date: Name: Contact details:

Do you wish your complaint to be anonymised? Yes No

Details of the complaint

How would you like to resolve the complaint?

Complaints Procedure.

*If you are using the service or have used the service in the past, you are able to make a com*plaint.

If you are still using the service, then you may choose to discuss your concern with your counsellor.

Any formal complaint will be managed by the Director. Formal complaints may be made via the above form, by telephone, or by email. Letter or in person.

Director - contact details:

Formal complaints will be investigated within a twenty-one-day period, and you will be contacted by letter with the outcome. Serious complaints may take up to four months to investigate and complete.

The next three forms are the questionnaires that your counsellor may or may not use with you. When they are used, it is normally at the beginning of the counselling and often, intermittently throughout the rest of the counselling. The questionnaires may be given to you to complete yourself or the counsellor may ask the questions and mark your answers on the questionnaires. They enable the counsellor to gain an appreciation of what you are experiencing and how best to proceed. They also show if you may need support promptly. Your counselling progress or setbacks can also be measured using these questionnaires. The forms may enable some clients to describe their experiences as well as help the counsellor to evaluate progress or lack of progress.

General Anxiety Disorder -seven

Generalised Anxiety Disorder is about your anxiety and comprises of seven questions. The answers are based on the last two weeks and consider worries and nervousness. The scores reveal symptoms from mild to severe. Below are the first few questions of the questionnaire. The scoring is based on zero to three, and the counsellor adds up the scores for each answer to make an assessment.

Over the last two weeks, how often have you been bothered by the following problems?

Scores -

Not at all zero Several Days one Over half the days two Nearly every day three

Feeling nervous, anxious, or on edge

Not being able to stop or control worrying

Patient Health Questionnaire – nine

This is about the severity of depression. There are nine questions in total, and each one pertains to a symptom of depression. Below are the first few questions. The scoring is based on one to four, and the counsellor adds up the scores for each answer to make an assessment.

Over the last two weeks, how often have you been bothered by the following problems?

Scores -

Not at all one Several days two More than half the days three Nearly Every day four

Little interest or pleasure in doing things

Feeling tired and having little energy

Clinical Outcomes in Routine Evaluation – ten

Clinical Outcomes in Routine Evaluation questionnaire is associated with several aspects, as well as anxiety and depression; it considers trauma, physical health and overall functioning. It helps to support, monitor and track progress. As the name implies, it has ten questions and below are the first few questions.

This form has ten statements about how you have been over the last week

Scores –

Not at all zero, only occasionally one, sometimes two Often three Most of the time four

Over the last week, I have felt tense, anxious, or nervous

I have felt I have someone to turn to for support when needed.

The final form is the Client Feedback Form, which is given to clients after they have finished their last counselling session. The form may be offered directly after the end of counselling or sent after a few weeks or a month after the counselling ended. Not all organisations or private counsellors will give out the feedback forms, but many do.

It is entirely up to you if you wish to complete and return the form or not. You may choose to answer some questions and not others, and you may choose to send the form back anonymously. Organisations and counsellors give out these forms for a variety of different reasons. Many counselling organisations are funded and receive lots of positive client feedback forms, which is often very useful for them to continue to be given funding. Some organisations and counsellors are genuinely interested in client feedback and comments.

I personally am not sure how useful these forms are, especially when given immediately after ending counselling. Clients may feel obliged to complete the forms positively as they do not wish to upset the counsellor. Some clients may feel good immediately after ending counselling and complete the form positively, but a month or so later, have regressed and would complete the form differently. The timing of giving these forms needs to be thoughtfully considered.

The Client Feedback forms vary enormously between organisations and private counsellors. Some may have, say, five questions and others up to twenty. Some may ask for 'yes or 'no' answers, others may ask for a score or one to ten and a few use words – strongly agree, agree, do not agree, do not know. The questions asked are often related to the main aspects that the organisation or counsellor wants feedback on specifically, rather than general questions related to important aspects of the counselling experience.

Brief examples are offered below.

Client Feedback Form One.

Name:

Date counselling ended:

Name of counsellor:

How many counselling sessions did you have?

Did your counsellor deliver a professional service?

How helpful was the counselling on a scale of one to ten, with ten being the most helpful?

(Circle one)

One two three four five six seven eight nine ten

How did you feel when you finished the counselling

(Circle one)

Really Good/ Good/ Not Good/

Client Feedback Form Two.

In a few words, please comment generally on aspects of your counselling experience -

How satisfied were you with the service overall on a scale of one to ten, with ten being the most satisfied?

(Circle one)

One Two Three Four Five Six Seven Eight Nine Ten

In a few words, please comment on your counsellor -

Any further comments -

Thank you for completing the form. Please return to: Counselling Service.

Just to let you know that there are also worksheets that some counsellors use for clients to complete in between sessions. They may be associated with different types of counselling and used for clients with anxiety and/or depression, amongst other client issues. Work sheets may be, for example, useful breathing exercises or situations to contemplate, coping skills, self-reflection or anxiety. A very brief example is below.

Anxiety Management Worksheet

Section one: *Identifying the Anxiety*

What triggered your anxiety today

What physical sensations did you notice?

Section Two: *Challenging Anxious Thoughts*

Is there evidence that supports this thought

Is there evidence that contradicts it

Section three: *Grounding Techniques*

Deep breathing: Inhale for 4, hold for 4, exhale for 4

Listen to calming music or nature sounds

It may feel to you that these forms are not necessary, but they are all essential. They enable the counsellor to help you by offering support and aiding the counselling process. The documentation can also help you to progress and generally enhance the process. The details in these documents will vary considerably, which is why I have only offered partial examples of the many documents used in counselling. These days, counsellors have more and more forms, documents and general administration to deal with for record keeping purposes and for client safety and also to enable the delivery and continuance of high-standard counselling. They safeguard the rights of clients and offer continuity of care and empowerment.

Try not to feel overwhelmed by the forms. If you are unsure about how to complete them, then ask the counsellor or organisation to help you. Assistance can be offered to vulnerable clients, especially. The forms can also be completed at the first counselling session. It is perfectly all right to feel tied in knots when trying to complete them. Put the forms to one side and contact the organisation or counsellor for help or ensure that you have them with you for your assessment or first session.

Personal Reflection.

I have always been careful and conscientious when it comes to handling documents, information, and records, as many of my colleagues are. *The attention to detail forms a large part of the training for counsellors and has become even more crucial in recent years. I once supervised a highly skilled counsellor whose work was excellent, and our sessions were always meaningful and productive. However, at the beginning of one session, she was very distressed. A client she had seen over several sessions had sadly died by their own hand. The counsellor was involved in the subsequent inquest because the client had been in contact with her shortly before their death. The coroner requested a statement and evidence from her. Unfortunately, she had not documented many of her sessions, nor had she fully acted on a risk assessment or safeguarding measures when the client disclosed suicidal thoughts.*

During the inquest, she was questioned about the client's disclosures, her understanding of the client's mental state, and the actions she had taken regarding risk and safeguarding. With little documentation to rely on, she could only share what she remembered. The coroner was naturally annoyed, and the counsellor received a reprimand. This sad situation highlights why thorough documentation is essential for everyone's safety and accountability.

In the time that followed, the counsellor was very upset over the client's death and felt guilt and embarrassment. I gave her ongoing emotional support for her to express her feelings and concerns without judgment. It reaffirmed the vital role of guidance and support in helping colleagues through difficult moments.

Information, records and documentation all help clients as well as counsellors. For clients, they clarify goals and progress, encourage reflection and communication. They provide continuity and enhance understanding. It assists in progress tracking, feedback, assessments and outcomes and can reassure clients that their information is managed carefully. They ensure that legal, ethical and professional standards are maintained. Poor documentation can cause legal liability, client harm and loss of trust. Documents must always be signed, and records must be accurate and complete.

Chapter Six
Counsellor Training

A Rigorous discipline or a Casual Pursuit?

'Counsellor training offers a challenging education not an indifferent pastime'

Over the years, counselling has become a widely recognised and effective way of supporting individuals with wellbeing and mental health concerns, and it has consequently grown in popularity. This rise in demand has led to a substantial expansion of counselling services and a significant increase in counsellortraining establishments, which continue to grow.

Counsellor training varies considerably, as do the course trainers. More experienced trainers can provide valuable mentorship to trainee counsellors, ensuring they are well-prepared for the future. These trainers should be able to offer trainees a solid foundation in both practical skills and theoretical knowledge, which is essential for offering high standards of counselling. Whilst there are many dedicated and professional counselling trainers offering excellent training, there are also many inferior trainers with minimal qualifications who are unable to offer quality training or consistently high standards.

Be aware that training may take three to four years on a parttime basis. Costs can be considerable, especially when factoring in personal therapy and supervision fees. The training requires resilience, as it can be intense and emotionally demanding. It involves a combination of study and practice, selfreflection and competence, ethics and empathy. A number of would-be trainee's stumble into counselling knowing very little about it.

Training Courses.

In order to offer a qualification in counselling, each training centre must be affiliated to an awarding body who set the standards and awards for the counselling courses. There are a large number of awarding bodies in the United Kingdom, although not all will offer counselling qualifications. Each awarding body that offers counselling qualifications may have a small or large number of counselling centres connected to it. The number of counselling trainees in each centre working on their final counselling qualification may be, on average, between ten and twenty for each individual course. It is fairly easy to work out that each year there are many hundreds of trainee counsellors who ultimately succeed in becoming qualified. This does not take into account those who qualify from university counselling courses.

Counsellor Training courses are held in a number of establishments, including universities, further education colleges, private organisations and more recently through online study courses. Universities have their own qualification whereas further education colleges and private centres will use awarding bodies for their qualifications. Their ways of working will all differ as will what is taught and the length of the courses. The therapeutic approaches chosen by the centres will be diverse and, most importantly, the quality of the teachers and teaching will contrast dramatically.

Stages of counsellor training.

Introduction Course – counselling skills to decide if counsellor training is for you. (eight to twelve weeks). The focus is on listening, communication and empathy.

Certificate Course – to develop skills, understand theories and communication. One year part-time. The focus is on skills, theories and ethics.

Diploma Course – for deeper all-round knowledge and practical training. Two years part-time. The focus is in depth study of theories and supervised practice. There will also be personal therapy and written assignments. Towards the end of the Diploma course, there will be placements where trainees work with clients.

Counsellor training centres will offer courses at different levels, for example, the first course is a level two, which will be a short introductory course running for up to ten weeks, usually one day a week. Level three will be a year in total, usually one day a week, and the final level is level four, which is normally two years of usually one day a week. Universities work generally on a modular basis. Trainees who choose to enter counsellor training will normally be looking at three years plus to complete and become qualified. Throughout the year, no teaching is offered during holiday periods.

For level four, there may be one or two residential weekends over the two-year period, but these are not mandatory. The cost of residential weekends may be part of the course cost or may have to be paid for by the counselling trainees. These weekends offer additional teaching in a variety of topics and are usually practical-based, where trainees can learn a great deal about themselves, counselling generally, and the various topics included in the residential weekends. If residential weekends are not offered, then the centre may put on non-residential weekend workshops, such as group work, mental health, mindfulness and suicidal ideation.

The two-year Level 4 counselling course includes a practical component, which may vary slightly depending on the awarding body. This involves a one-year placement at a counselling organisation, during which trainee counsellors must complete a minimum of 100 client sessions. The counselling trainees must carry out these placement hours in their own time. All client work must be supervised by a qualified counselling supervisor, and supervision sessions are also arranged between the centre and the trainee. In some cases, the cost of supervision may be covered within the course fees, and if not, trainees will have to pay for these sessions themselves. Supervision generally takes place once or twice a month.

It is strongly recommended that trainee counsellors engage in personal therapy during their training. This helps them to address their own issues and provides an opportunity to experience being in the position of a client. However, not all training centres require personal therapy to be undertaken outside of course hours. The experience offers trainees the opportunity to gain self-awareness, increased confidence and competence. Learning will encompass empathy, active listening and questioning. Ethics and boundaries will be introduced together with responsibility, confidentiality and reflective practice.

Personal Reflection.

My work as a counsellor trainer in three different establishments has enabled me to appreciate the importance of counsellors undertaking their own personal counselling. *In one centre, it was mandatory for trainee counsellors to engage in personal counselling. In the other two centres, it was not mandatory; one took a more relaxed approach, leaving it up to the trainees to decide if they wanted to participate or not. In the other, it was not part of the curriculum. I firmly believe that personal counselling is an important part of counsellor training as it offers an opportunity for trainee* *counsellors to learn about themselves and to appreciate what it feels like to be in the client's position.*

Towards the end of these courses, the difference between trainee counsellors who had personal counselling and those who had not was obvious. While I appreciate both the time and money involved, I believe that all counselling training centres should make personal counselling mandatory for trainees.

Throughout counsellor training, there will be an amalgamation of theory, skills practice and personal development. During the two years on the level four counsellor training course, trainees will have to complete several assignments which are assessed by the trainers. The assignments are varied, and each one is related to a taught aspect of the course. Trainees must pass each assignment offered in the course. Once all the assignments have been completed and passed, and the one hundred supervised client hours have been attained, the trainee produces an externally assessed portfolio, which will vary from one training centre and awarding body to another.

The portfolios require high standards and an excellent understanding of the evidence required. Every aspect in the portfolio must be sufficient to pass. The portfolio will be assessed by examiners/assessors from the course's awarding body. If the portfolio is a pass, it enables the trainee to become a qualified counsellor.

Bear in mind that trainee counsellors, working their one hundred client hours, often use case studies for their final portfolios. Clients used for these case studies must have been asked for their permission in the first instance. It is necessary when permissions are requested for case studies that a client signature, on an appropriate form, is obtained. You have every right to refuse.

The Training.

Each counsellor training centre will have its own methods of accepting trainees onto the courses. This means that most, if not all, trainees who apply and complete an application form will be accepted, even though some of them may be unsuitable. All sorts of people, who truly wish to help others, will be admitted onto the courses with counselling trainers not really knowing the abilities or inadequacies of the counsellor trainees. At the very least, potential trainees should be self-aware, committed and have several personal qualities. Such qualities would be good communication and interpersonal skills, patience and compassion, empathy and self-awareness. These qualities cannot be taught.

The counselling trainers.

There are aspects of counsellor training that differ significantly from many other forms of education. Highly experienced and qualified trainers with teaching qualifications are essential. They must be fully qualified counsellors with significant counselling experience. They should also continue working with clients and receive supervision for this clinical work. In reality, some counsellor trainers no longer engage in client work, and only a few possess formal teaching qualifications. In private training centres, teaching qualifications are not always required.

Teaching counselling is quite different from teaching other subjects. It requires flexibility, imagination, creativity, and a deep understanding of both theory and practice, along with the ability to communicate these effectively to trainees. They should offer trainees theoretical and practical examples and demonstrations, as they need to have lots of assistance during their skills practices and theory sessions. As part of the Level 4 course, there will be personal development groups facilitated by an experienced group trainer. This is an important aspect of a trainee counsellor's development as these groups share and debate such things as beliefs and values, strengths and weaknesses, attitudes, styles and standards.

The working relationship between trainer and trainees should be a professional and not an overly friendly one. Trainers also have the task of marking trainees' assignments and offering help when they do not meet the required standard. Trainers should regularly monitor or review their own courses and teaching practice, for example, checking sufficient creativity, integrity, competence and principles. They should also consider adequate support and mentoring for trainees. All trainees must be offered comprehensive teaching, especially in theory and skills.

Examiners and Moderators.

Examiners

Awarding bodies work with external independent examiners and moderators. They designate the examiners to assess the students' final and external portfolios. The final portfolios will differ from one awarding body to another in terms of the contents. External examiners, as the name implies, work from home and assess the final portfolio or examination papers that ultimately enable trainee counsellors to become qualified. Usually, each awarding body, depending upon how many counselling centres they offer awards to, will have several examiners. These examiners will have regular standardisation meetings to ensure that they are all assessing the work objectively, correctly, consistently and conforming to the standard. All offering similar constructive feedback for any aspects that are referred to. The chosen examiners should be counsellor trainers and practising counsellors.

A percentage of portfolios do not pass the first time, some because pages have been omitted or there are no signatures where there should be, some trainees have simply not provided the appropriate evidence or have not understood what evidence is required. Apart from these, a proportion of referred portfolios are simply substandard, and some have plagiarised other students' or authors' work. This is the most important element of their training that enables them to pass and become a qualified counsellor. Offering inferior work, missed pages, no signatures and copied aspects is totally unacceptable. It shows a lack of care and attention, irresponsibility and negligence. It is unfortunate that some awarding bodies offer trainees several additional re-takes.

Personal Reflection.

I am only able to offer examples of the malpractice and incompetence that I have been aware of, but it still makes very interesting reading *for a profession that encompasses such strict ethical guidelines and cares about the well-being of clients. I have assessed many final portfolios of trainee counsellors where it is obvious that signatures have been forged. This situation is often found when an original part of the portfolio has been referred and the resubmitted evidence has been amended. Other records that have been obviously modified have been the final placement or supervisor reports.*

Plagiarism is a popular one, either copying another trainee counsellor's work or copying directly from counselling books. Both of which I have come across frequently. It saddens me to think that these trainee counsellors can go to such lengths to try to pass their final portfolio. They are a far cry from the professional, ethical and competent counsellors who have worked intently and honestly and made great efforts to pass and become qualified counsellors.

Moderators.

Awarding bodies designate moderators to liaise with the centres. Often, but not always, travelling to centres to assess each level of counselling training that the centres offer. They talk to the counselling trainers, assess all the documentation, answer questions and offer advice. They normally talk to some of the students to check their experience of the training. The moderators also sample a number of the students' internally marked assignments to check that the marking is objective and consistent. Forms are completed and an assessment made as to whether the centre can continue or whether sanctions need to be put in place. The one or two visits to each centre each year can last for many hours, as it is a thorough appraisal of the centre and its training. Some moderation visits have been reduced firstly to just one visit a year, and for those centres considered above average, reduced to postal/email appraisals.

Job opportunities.

Not all the newly qualified counsellors will choose to practice counselling, and of those who do wish to practice counselling, not all will be fortunate enough to secure employment as counsellors. There are many more opportunities for counsellors these days, but the number of newly qualified counsellors far exceeds the number of available jobs. Employers want more than the basic counselling qualification from their prospective employees. Most employers require counsellors to be qualified and experienced, which has prompted a number of counselling training centres to offer post qualification training courses on counselling specialisms. Employers also require counsellors to be accredited by a professional body.

The job market is currently competitive, and often positions are only sessional. Accreditation requires strict standards for the training courses, such as a minimum of 450 trainer contact hours. Counsellors must have at least 450 client hours over three to six years. Many counsellors are not accredited, and I would advise you to ensure that you choose a counsellor who is accredited. Becoming accredited improves professional credibility and ultimately client trust. It indicates high standards of practice.

Statutory Regulation.

Most healthcare professions have to be registered with the appropriate regulator under statutory healthcare regulation. The regulators set standards of competence and check the quality of training courses; they maintain a register and will investigate complaints. The government has been debating the statutory regulation of counsellors for over two decades, and at the time of writing, it currently has no plans to put this into action. However, it is an ongoing topic in the UK, and it is gaining more attention. Statutory regulation means that counsellors and psychotherapists would be legally required to register with a government -approved body. This would protect their professional titles, ensure that minimum standards of ethics, training and conduct are met. Importantly, misconduct would also be investigated by regulatory bodies. Professional bodies have accredited voluntary registers, and counsellors can join the organisation and obtain a certificate of proficiency. Voluntary bodies like BACP and UKCP can suspend or expel members, but they are unable to stop someone from continuing to practice.

Finally.

Good trainers would be aware of the many aspects of counsellor training and would have a thorough knowledge of the entire course. They should be able to offer quality teaching and be capable of motivating students. The ability to structure a course is crucial, as is timing, planning and working with different student learning styles. The potential to keep the sessions interesting and be aware of group dynamics is essential. Giving constructive feedback and handling difficult trainees is paramount. Communication and presentation skills are also necessary. They should set clear objectives and encourage self-development. Ethical practice must be taught and evaluating trainee's skills practice.

Poor trainers will be poor role models; they will offer conflicting ethical guidance, outdated information, insufficient motivation and reduced skills practice, resulting in restricted personal growth and a lack of competence. This can lead to negative outcomes for clients in the long run. Counsellor training can be a rich and exciting journey with good trainers managing the courses, offering quality education and professional development. The trainees will gain insight and maturity and will have a sound understanding of clients' experiences and feelings.

Chapter Seven

Pick Or Mix

An Abundance of Theoretical Approaches

'Theoretical approaches reflect the importance of theory in practice, the role of the counsellor is understanding and applying them.'

I will offer a brief overview of some of the main theories within counselling. There are over four hundred theoretical approaches, a bewildering number, with some being complex and confusing. Many of these approaches are not widely known, and others continue to emerge. However, they all rely, in some way, on aspects of the original theories.

A counselling theory, often described as a model or approach, forms the foundation or framework that counsellors use as an essential part of the counselling process. Each theory acts like a roadmap or sat-nav, offering direction by using the knowledge and skills of those who developed and practised it. Once a theory is understood, it will offer clarity to the counselling. The theory guides the counselling process, helping counsellors to understand your issues and support your well-being. Regardless of differences in all the theories, they will all help different clients, albeit in different ways.

Many potential clients may not realise that counselling practice is underpinned by specific theories. It is important to ask a counsellor about the theory that they use or the theories they are trained in. They should be able to explain their theoretical approach clearly. Each theory has its own background, principles, and concepts, and will work with client issues in different ways.

There is no evidence to suggest that one approach is superior to another, as all aim to help clients. Some counsellors use a single approach, while others integrate more than one theory. A theory helps to guide the counsellor in how best to support you.

When prospective counsellors search for a training centre, they should consider the theory or theories that the centre uses as the basis of its training. They should feel comfortable with the theoretical approach offered before committing. However, many seem to accept whatever is available. Most centres choose approaches that their trainers are familiar with. Some focus on a single theory to ensure that trainees gain a thorough understanding, whilst offering only a brief overview of other theories. This is good practice, as theories can be complex, requiring a counselling trainer to be knowledgeable of the theory or theories and the ability to put them into practice.

Some centres offer multiple theories, which can reduce the time spent on each. Offering three theories is becoming more common, and while this may sound appealing, the limited time available at the final level of training means only a few students actually leave understanding all three. Three theories could lead to quantity over quality. A thorough understanding of one theoretical approach is far more valuable than a weak knowledge of several approaches.

It is important to ask the counsellor what theory or theories they use and to explain how these guide their work. Different approaches and different styles may be offered as some theories focus on exploring your past, others on changing current behaviours or thought patterns. No single theory will fit all clients. What matters most is how well the approach suits your needs and how skilled the counsellor is in using it.

Be cautious with newer theories, as some may not suit your needs, but it may be worth asking questions to make sure that you feel comfortable if it is a new theory.

I have chosen some theoretical approaches to briefly outline for you; these are some of the most popular, each one has its own unique methods and goals.

Psychoanalysis

I will begin with Freud, a name most will have heard of. Sigmund Freud developed psychoanalysis in the late nineteenth century. The theory is based on unconscious thoughts and perceptions developed during childhood and the impact these have on behaviour and thoughts as an adult. Psychoanalysis continues today, but many of the ideas that Freud developed have been adapted and changed. Whilst there are counsellors who still offer psychoanalysis, many will use the more popular Psychodynamic counselling.

Psychodynamic

This form of counselling has its roots in psychoanalysis. However, it is shorter than the psychoanalytical approach and not as intense. Its focus is on past experiences and unconscious patterns. It explores how early relationships and unresolved conflicts shape your current behaviour. It helps uncover hidden emotions and patterns that may be affecting your life today. It looks at a client's past to help find solutions for present issues. It helps in understanding and resolving deep-seated emotional concerns and can be used for depression and anxiety, addictions and eating disorders as well as other issues. It can be a longer-term form of counselling.

Behavioural

This theory originated from Pavlov's classical conditioning and Skinner's operant conditioning. It looks at changing unwanted behaviour using the belief that behaviour is learnt and can be unlearnt, and uses operant and/or classical conditioning. It focuses on changing unhealthy ways through techniques like reinforcement and punishment, desensitization and aversion therapy to help modify unhealthy behaviours. It is effective for disorders like obsessive compulsive disorder, attention deficit hyperactive disorder and specific phobias.

There are still behavioural counsellors today. However, in the main, it is the more accessible cognitive behavioural therapy that is being used to a greater extent. In the nineteen fifties and nineteen sixties, Albert Ellis developed behavioural therapy, and Aaron Beck developed cognitive therapy, respectively. The two combined their work, which emerged as Cognitive Behavioural Therapy, which became more widespread in the nineteen nineties onwards.

Cognitive Behavioural Therapy

The focus of this therapy is on thoughts, feelings, and behaviours. It helps you notice and change unhelpful thinking patterns. If you often feel anxious or stuck in negative cycles, cognitive behavioural therapy teaches practical strategies to challenge negative thinking. It is currently a really popular short-term therapy and is utilised a great deal by the National Health Service. Being short-term, it is cost-effective and is also offered by the National Health Service online. It uses in-session exercises and homework exercises to enable clients to alter their thoughts, feelings and behaviour by acquiring coping strategies. The emphasis is on what clients want to achieve rather than on clients discussing past issues. It is used mainly for anxiety and depression, phobias and more. It teaches practical skills to manage stress and improve mental health.

Person Centred Therapy

Non-directive therapy was developed by Carl Rogers in the nineteen forties. It was subsequently renamed Client-Centred Therapy. It began to gain popularity through the nineteen fifties and nineteen sixties. Later, the name was changed again, this time to Person Centred Therapy. The focus is on empathy, acceptance, and self-growth. This approach believes you already have the inner resources to grow and heal. The counsellor offers a warm, non-judgmental space where you feel truly heard. Over time, this helps you reconnect with your strengths and values. It emphasises personal growth and self-fulfilment and has become one of the most widely used therapeutic approaches. It looks at how clients perceive themselves and how all clients have the ability to achieve what they wish to achieve. It encompasses responsibility and self-development; it empowers, motivates and enables clients. It is one of the most popular theoretical approaches used by counsellors. This form of counselling can be helpful for almost all issues such as anxiety, relationships, post-traumatic stress and depression, among others. It enables self-awareness and personal development. It helps clients to achieve their full potential.

Gestalt

Developed by Fritz and Laura Perls in the nineteen forties, Gestalt Therapy looks at how clients can be more aware and integrated. It derives from psychoanalysis and existential philosophy. It works with thoughts and emotions, and also includes spiritual and body experiences and minute-to-minute awareness. An experiential therapy that focuses on the present and personal responsibility. It uses the here and now and self-discovery, enabling calm, self-confidence and peace. It is appropriate for many psychological challenges, emphasising personal responsibility and using techniques like role-playing to help clients become more aware of their thoughts and feelings. It can help with issues such as anxiety and low self-esteem, among others; it may not be suitable for all clients.

Transactional Analysis

This theory was developed by Eric Berne in the late nineteen fifties. It is a theory rooted in psychoanalysis and works on transactions or communications between people. It is essentially a model of people and relationships. It focuses on results by concentrating on social interactions as the source of the client's issues. Transactional Analysis helps to develop self-awareness and more effective decision-making. It identifies interactions that are not productive to enable improved relationships and personal growth. It can help with issues such as phobias, depression and relationship difficulties, among others.

Integrative Therapy.

This is a combination of several theories. The focus is on combining approaches to suit each client. Some counsellors combine techniques from different theories to match a client's unique needs. This might include elements of cognitive behavioural therapy, person-centred, and psychodynamic therapy. I have no problem at all with this approach providing the counsellor has more than an average knowledge of each theory and how they should be applied in practice. Unfortunately, from my experience and, as previously mentioned, three or more theories are being taught in the final training year, which results in insufficient teaching time for trainees to fully understand, appreciate and apply all the theories. Qualifying in one theoretical approach makes more sense, and then adding on another one or two approaches through continued professional development over another year or two would be more logical, giving time to become fully aware of which aspects of each approach to apply with each individual client.

Integrative counsellors propose that one theory does not fit, which is reasonable, but I suggest that it is more about the counsellor and their skills, qualities, experience and knowledge that matter the most and not how many theoretical approaches they are trained in.

These counselling theories are just a few of the more conventional ones practised. Today, however, many more theories exist; not all are being extensively practised, they vary considerably, and many are vague and meaningless. Counselling is a developing profession with new theories being introduced, which offer new ideas. Some of these are established on the principles of traditional theoretical approaches. Their usefulness is dependent on the issue(s) that clients bring to counselling. These new approaches must be considered carefully. I question if all the theories, both traditional and modern, actually constitute richness or clutter.

Some new theories can offer innovative ways to help counsellors with complex challenges. They can be empowering and can work well, integrating with other traditional theories. The new theoretical approaches do have limitations and some lack validation. Counsellors will require further education to understand and implement them. Not all new clients will be prepared to accept new theoretical approaches.

Theories are important; they offer a framework for understanding clients, without them, counselling would be impromptu and inconsistent. They guide counselling interventions and help to interpret complex situations. They can assist with establishing trust and improving the counsellor's skills. Without theories, there would be a lack of direction and ethical issues. They are the foundation of effective practice.

As a prospective client, you should understand the theory that the counsellor works with, which they should fully explain to you. It is useful to explore different theories and get a sense of which one resonates with you. Finding a counsellor and a theoretical approach that feels right can be very helpful. Consider the brief list above to identify which approach may best suit your issue(s). Check with prospective counsellors regarding the theoretical approaches that they use. You may prefer a theory with a structured approach or one that is short-term or long-term, perhaps a more relaxed one. Finding one that suits you and your issue(s) is essential and will crucially improve your counselling experience.

Counsellors must have thorough knowledge, understanding and appreciation of the theoretical approaches they use, along with the skills and interventions those theories support. Counselling is an interaction that involves a comprehensive understanding of the theoretical approach or approaches that the counsellor will use.

A theoretical approach provides the framework for understanding the entire counselling process. It determines the appropriate interventions and methods to use. Different therapeutic approaches are linked to different client issues. Explaining the counselling theory, what it is and how it works, helps clients feel at ease and builds trust.

As a counselling client, you will be expending your time and your emotional energy in the counselling and, as such, a competent counsellor is essential. It is crucial that counsellors are fully knowledgeable in one or more theoretical approaches and that they can explain the approach they use in a meaningful way without using counselling jargon. Understanding the theory will help you to feel informed, empowered and connected. It may be useful to explain your requirements to the counsellor to help them to find the right approach for you. Be aware that different approaches will achieve results at different rates.

Theories direct practice by offering structured ways to understand, predict and inform clients. Understanding the basics of the approach will enable you to engage more in the sessions. The framework of some of the theoretical approaches can offer fresh perspectives in the client work. It is important that counsellors choose the correct therapeutic approach for each individual client, together with the selection of skills and interventions that the theoretical approach(s) offer in order to support their well-being.

Some modern approaches and newer theories may sound appealing but lack strong scientific backing. That does not mean they are ineffective; just be sure your counsellor can explain how the approach works and why it is suitable for you. Understanding the theory behind the counselling will give you confidence and clarity. Ask about the theory, how it may help and how it works.

Chapter Eight
Supervision Or Visionless

Necessary and Mandatory Guidance

'From oversight to insight, supervision is ethical practice using dialogue.'

It is imperative for all counsellors to incorporate supervision into their counselling work, regardless of whether they have considerable or limited experience. Supervision is considered good ethical practice, and all counselling professional bodies ensure that registered counsellors undertake supervision regularly. This means that counsellors must engage the services of another, more experienced counsellor who is qualified to provide supervision. You should ask prospective counsellors whether they are supervised and request details of their supervisory arrangements. A supervisor acts as an unbiased consultant for counsellors. Supervision should be conducted ethically and thoroughly to safeguard clients. It ensures quality, maintains standards, provides support and offers counsellors a reflective space. It is essential, as it confirms that a counsellor is working professionally and to a high standard of practice.

What is supervision?

Supervision enables counsellors to remain grounded and to enhance their practical and theoretical understanding. It ensures that they are practising ethically and within their boundaries. It is supportive as well as challenging and should include all aspects of counselling practice, how counsellors relate to clients and the counsellor's own process based on their thoughts and feelings relating to client work. Counselling supervision is similar to having a mentor to help counsellors to improve and to ensure that their clients receive the highest standards of care. The aim is for the counsellor to develop creativity and confidence, which results in competent client work.

Counselling supervision provides counsellors with professional development. It is where a counsellor meets with a qualified supervisor, usually monthly, to reflect on their work, gain guidance and ensure they are providing the best possible support to their clients. Supervisors will discuss challenges that the counsellor may be facing, and they will review the counsellor's techniques and ways of working. The counsellor will request guidance, reflect on their work and gain insight through constructive feedback.

Supervision is a safe place and a good learning experience where there is no judgment. For the counsellor, supervision will ensure that they are working proficiently and safely and within their own limitations. The supervisor will monitor how the counsellor is facilitating the client's progress, evaluating the counsellor's competence and ensuring that their counselling is beneficial, that they are undertaking continued professional development and are offering clients a high standard of professional and ethical practice. Counsellors should ensure that you are made aware of the role that supervision plays, as this will provide you with confidence. They should explain that supervision is ultimately for your benefit.

Supervision and confidentiality.

During the course of supervision, some details from the client's counselling sessions are shared with the supervisor to ensure that the counsellor is working in the best interests of the clients. These shared aspects relate to the counsellor's progress, rather than the clients themselves. It is the counsellor's responsibility to inform you about confidentiality in supervision. You should be made aware that your identifying information is not disclosed to the supervisor and that anything shared or explored during counselling sessions is protected under the contract of confidentiality. Any information must not be disclosed outside of supervision, except in relation to a court order. Client confidentiality remains paramount in supervision. Counsellors must never share identifiable information unless the client has given consent. Supervisors are also bound by confidentiality and must not disclose any information discussed during supervision sessions. There are exceptions to confidentiality, such as confidentiality may be breached in supervision if there is a risk of serious harm to a client or others, if there is a legal obligation, such as court orders or if the client has consented to disclosures. Supervision is an ongoing process for counsellors.

Personal Reflection

When I was training students who were working in placements and attending regular supervision*, we held study sessions to consider and discuss supervision more generally. On many occasions, I heard students talking about their clients and client work during these sessions. I had to remind them that all client work is confidential, and I had to firmly explain that this constituted a breach of confidentiality. In future sessions, client details were no longer mentioned.*

Later, I became aware, through other supervisors, that some qualified counsellors had also shared client work and personal details with their colleagues, which is unethical and unprofessional. Offering clients confidentiality and then sharing their information with others breaches both ethical codes and the General Data Protection Regulation.

Confidentiality is an essential aspect of a safe and trusting counselling relationship. Supervisors should always explain to the counsellors that confidentiality should be made clear and discussed with clients during their first counselling session.

Supervisors – training and practice.

As with training to become a counsellor, not everyone is suitable to become a supervisor. That does not, however, stop people from becoming supervisors. All supervisors must have undergone a supervisor training course, but unfortunately, not all those who practice supervision have done so. Many consider that their years of counselling experience is sufficient for offering supervision. It appears to most that offering supervision is a natural progression for counsellors, but actually, it requires another set of skills from counselling skills. Whilst experience is extremely helpful, it is essential to have undergone supervision training in order to understand what is required as supervisors, exactly what supervision is and how it is practised in order to enable counsellors to offer the best possible counselling to clients. Supervisors must have knowledge of the traits and qualities required of supervisors, such as management skills and intervention skills.

Supervision courses were once few and far between, but they now seem to have increased significantly. An increase in counsellors may be one reason, or perhaps it is simply because supervision has become a lucrative field. Good supervisors are almost as difficult to find as good counsellors. It is considered best practice for counsellors to have several years of counselling experience before embarking on a supervision training course. Good counsellors will check the credentials and experience of prospective supervisors and will work only with the best.

How much supervision is required?

Professional bodies usually offer the requirements for supervision, although these will vary from one body to another. There is usually a set amount that is generally accepted for trainee counsellors. This is a monthly supervision of one and a half hours minimum for up to twelve client hours of counselling. This amounts to seeing three clients a week for a month, which is acceptable for trainees. I know for certain that many trainee counsellors want to achieve their total number of hours needed to qualify in the shortest possible time. This translates to seeing more than three clients in a week in their counselling placements, which should ideally not happen. Alternatively, they find a second placement to see another three clients a week, which would mean that their supervision hours should be doubled. I have assessed trainee counsellor portfolios where a few trainees have four counselling placements. This is not acceptable, but is allowed by awarding bodies.

For qualified counsellors, the amount of supervision seems to be relaxed a little and is dependent upon the number of client hours, the counsellor's experience, the counselling settings and the complexity of the work. The one and a half hours a month should still stand as a minimum. This, however, should always be discussed with the supervisor. A record of all supervision hours should be maintained for trainees and qualified counsellors. I am aware of qualified counsellors who do not have supervision at all; some who have supervision as and when they feel they need it; some who have casual chats with colleagues and call it supervision.

There are different types of supervision, the main and most beneficial type being on a one-to-one basis, that is, all the supervision time for one counsellor to use. Another type of supervision is group supervision, which is one supervisor with anything from three to six counsellors. For me, this is not an ideal situation, as often not every counsellor has time to bring their issues and the more people in the group, the longer the group will have to meet. This is an accepted form for trainee counsellors, but not one that I endorse, as trainees need all the individual time they can get for their supervision. It is a good addition to having one-to-one supervision, but even this can raise concerns in terms of sharing the same client with both one-to-one and group supervisors, resulting in differences of opinion and confusion for the counsellor. It is more accepted for qualified counsellors, but one counsellor bringing two or three issues could take up time, leaving other counsellors unable to bring their issues. There can be difficulties with group dynamics and also with finding a supervisor who is experienced in working with groups.

Yet another form of supervision is peer supervision, which can take place between two or more counsellors. Again, this is a good addition to monthly one-to-one supervision, but not good when used on its own. It is not suitable at all for trainee counsellors. There is no supervisor present in these groups, and the counsellors work out their contract and way of working between themselves. The counsellors have to be quite fixed on the task of supervision, or, as so easily can happen, the time is taken up with catching and discussion on counselling generally. There is often a variation in attendance for these groups. I personally would only be interested in supervising a counsellor having regular one-to-one supervision.

Personal Reflection.

Challenge is an important part of supervision, where counsellors are challenged to reflect on elements of their client work. *I had a supervisee whom I had been working with for over six* *months, during which I used gentle challenges when appropriate. Her client list began to grow in number and also in complexity, and, as such, more challenge was essential. When challenged, she became quite defensive and belligerent. I took time out to explain*

the reasoning behind the challenge, to no avail. We continued our supervision sessions for a few months, with her being argumentative. After further discussion, she ended her supervision with me and, no doubt, sought another supervisor who probably did not challenge.

Yet another would be a counsellor, who was a friend of a colleague of mine, who asked me to be her supervisor. I had a discussion with her and would have taken her on until she asked if I would sign off on client hours that had not been supervised for the past several months. I declined and explained how unethical this would be. She did eventually qualify a short time later, and I guess that she found a less-than-ethical supervisor who would sign these hours for her without supervising them.

Effective supervision will lead to effective counselling. All counsellors, whether in training or experienced, need to regularly take their client work to supervision to enable them to continue to work with clients in a safe and helpful way. The importance of supervision is essential for trainee counsellors and experienced counsellors alike. Supervision ensures sustained counsellor development, high counselling standards and good quality client care. Counsellors can process their thoughts and experiences in supervision, and the supervisor can verify that they are working to ethical guidelines and are competent. You are within your rights to ask about a counsellor's supervision, how many hours and how often. Remember that supervision protects you by helping to lower the risk of counsellor mistakes.

What you should know as a counselling client.

- You should know that supervision is a confidential, ethical process that protects your well-being and ensures high-quality care.
- Your identity is protected as supervisors do not receive identifying information about you. Supervision is bound by the same ethical standards as counselling, including confidentiality. Information shared in supervision is not disclosed outside of that space unless required by law (e.g., court order).
- Supervision ensures your counsellor is working in your best interest. That they are grounded, supported, and accountable.
- You are entitled to ask the counsellor if they have supervision and what confidentiality is. A good counsellor will explain these and reassure you.

Personal Reflection.

I have had the pleasure of supervising, over the years, a large number of qualified counsellors. Most have been very efficient, willing to learn and grow as counsellors. Some have brought complex issues asking for assistance, and others have requested understanding about their concerns with a distressed client. Others, mainly trainee counsellors, have been quiet and nervous, and a small number lacked interest.

Most of the qualified counsellors brought interesting issues and gained a lot from our sessions. Those with complex issues were eager to learn and, over the sessions, made very good progress. The counsellors who brought concerns with distressed clients took longer to appreciate client distress and how to deal with it, but over time, they began to understand and appreciate how to proceed. Some of the quiet and nervous counsellors became confident and assertive. Those who lacked interest ultimately left the counselling course.

During supervision sessions, counsellors can learn a great deal from self-reflection and ethical practice, to emotional support and the development of skills. Supervision helps counsellors to maintain high standards of practice. It is not just about offering direction and guidance; it is a place for counsellors to reflect and become more effective and resilient counsellors in a safe environment. They present cases, ask questions and discuss development. All of this is for the benefit of clients, as these professional counsellors who have regular supervision will offer high standards of counselling.

Supervision is the foundation for effective development. It monitors counsellors' performance and ensures responsibilities are being met by counsellors. It is a space for counsellors to reflect and make continuous improvements.

Effective supervisors will inspire, challenge, and support counsellors. It can feel a bit of a mystery to clients, but it is actually a powerful safeguard.

As a client, you benefit from supervision even though you never meet the supervisor. As it confirms that the counsellor is working ethically and effectively. Supervisors offer insights that ultimately improve client care.

Chapter Nine
The Erosion Of Ethical Accountability

A collapse of conscience

'The biggest threat to responsibility and accountability is the decline and neglecting of ethics and principles'

For counsellors, the word professional would indicate having specialised knowledge and being well-trained and experienced with a good understanding of therapeutic approaches and a range of skills and interventions. Their qualifications and counselling practice should determine their proficiency. A professional counsellor should take responsibility for their actions, be aware of their mistakes and learn from them. They should belong to a professional body and observe their ethical code. In addition, it is important for a counsellor to be adequately insured, to maintain accurate records, have regular supervision and be responsible and accountable.

Not all counsellors respect these important aspects and, in such cases, they are not working in a professional manner. The term professional carries expectations of expertise, respect, and ethical conduct. When counsellors fail to meet these standards, it may create uncertainty and dissatisfaction, as well as raise worries about clients' well-being. It is essential for qualified and professional counsellors to adhere to all of these elements. By understanding and recognising these key aspects, you will be better equipped to choose a counsellor who upholds high standards rather than one who relies on hollow words.

Accountability & Responsibility.

Accountability is being answerable for outcomes, actions and decisions. Counsellors must be honest and open with clients, explaining expectations, the therapeutic approach and methods of working. Mistakes must be acknowledged and action taken to correct them. Counsellors are accountable to clients for providing safe, respectful and effective counselling. They are responsible for safeguarding and data protection; maintaining records and legal compliance.

Responsibility is ensuring that all responsibilities are accomplished. Counsellors must work safely and effectively, in the client's best interests, providing security and productive counselling. They are required to maintain their expertise, knowledge, skills, and competence and to recognise their personal limitations. This includes engaging in regular supervision and continued professional development. Priorities are client welfare, competence, informed consent and transparency.

Taking on the role of a counsellor involves being reliable, trustworthy, open, and honest. It requires a strong sense of duty towards clients and a commitment to working in the best possible way with each individual. Upholding ethical standards and professionalism is essential. Counsellors who neglect these ethical principles put the integrity of the profession into question.

Ethical Principles.

The ethical principles give counsellors a framework to work within. Parts of the framework include cultural awareness, listening attentively to clients, respect for client autonomy, integrity, self-respect and avoiding causing harm.

They are the foundation for building trust and for the welfare of clients. The professional bodies provide the ethical frameworks.

Their code of ethics sets out the values and principles on which the profession is based, a set of rules that counsellors should read, understand and implement. Good counsellors should be familiar with at least one code of ethics.

Ethical codes offer guidance to training centres, trainee counsellors and supervisors. You should be aware that those counsellors who do not belong to a professional body may or may not abide by any code of ethics. Ethical responsibility is about upholding principles, for example, informed consent, client welfare, confidentiality and integrity to ascertain client welfare. Ethics apply to acting in the best interests of you, as a client; they are your protection, confirming that the counsellor observes and applies these principles for your well-being.

Professional Bodies.

To belong to a professional body, a counsellor would have to have a minimum qualification of a level four Diploma. There are some professional bodies that require a qualification higher than a level four Diploma. A few professional bodies have begun to offer self-regulation (upholding standards). Most also provide accredited registers for counsellors, which verify that these counsellors have met their requirements.

Counsellors do not have to become members of professional bodies, but there are advantages to membership. The advantage of belonging to a professional body means a counsellor will be offered a wide range of benefits. These would increase their practice and credibility. Continued professional development will be offered through workshops, seminars, courses and conferences and a range of resources such as journals and research papers. Some professional bodies can offer legal advice and reduced insurance.

Complaints.

As a counselling client, it is important to know that you have the right to make a complaint. There are many valid reasons why you might choose to do so. Complaints occur for a variety of issues; some examples may be that the counselling sessions have no structure or direction, resulting in a lack of progress or poor listening, where you feel you are not being heard. Perhaps the counsellor is judgmental or over-familiar. The counsellor may not offer warmth or empathy, making you feel belittled. There could be confidentiality concerns leading to broken trust or frequent cancellations and lateness by the counsellor. Not explaining the process to you or providing poor feedback. Counsellors who are not abiding by their ethical principles are doing a disservice to the profession and causing harm to clients.

Any concerns that you may have will be valid, and it is essential to try to resolve the issue directly. You can speak with the counsellor or the counselling organisation

If the issue cannot be resolved informally, you may need to follow a formal complaints procedure. If this does not bring about a resolution, then follow the complaints procedure.

This usually involves an acknowledgement of your complaint, an investigation of it and a decision being made based on the outcome. Whatever your concern, whether minor or significant, it is important to raise it and follow through. Doing so not only supports your own well-being but may also help others in similar situations. Complaints help to support and improve counselling services.

Insurance.

Similar to any other business, all counsellors must take out insurance. Several types of insurance should be considered, and these are often available as a package. Insurance provides protection against risks. Counsellors without insurance are irresponsible and unprofessional. While employed counsellors are usually covered by their organisation's insurance, those working independently require, at the very least, professional liability insurance. Having insurance demonstrates professionalism and offers a sense of security. Professional liability insurance should cover both public liability and professional indemnity. In addition to liability insurance, which protects against compensation claims, counsellors should also consider business premises insurance and income protection insurance.

The risks associated with counselling are completely different from those in other professions. Therefore, insurance must meet the specific needs of the counsellors. Malpractice insurance covers mental and psychological damage and is essential. Check that a counsellor has insurance cover. All responsible counsellors will maintain comprehensive insurance policies.

Even the most skilled counsellors can face allegations of professional negligence, breach of confidentiality, or ethical misconduct. Insurance, especially professional indemnity insurance, ensures that if something goes wrong, clients can take legal action without relying solely on the counsellor's personal resources. Having insurance demonstrates that the counsellor takes their duty of care seriously.

Continued professional development.

It is really important for counsellors to maintain good practice by developing their knowledge and skills and keeping up to date with standards. Accredited counsellors have to provide evidence of their continued professional development each year to preserve their accreditation status. All good professional counsellors must engage in continued professional development on a regular basis. It enables counsellors to carry on providing good, high-quality counselling. should be undertaken once counsellors have formally qualified.

The amount of continued professional development that should be gained each year varies, with some professional bodies expecting a minimum of twenty to thirty hours a year. It takes the form of, for example, attending conferences, reading books and journals, e-learning, workshops and training courses. Some counsellors are interested in specific areas of counselling and become skilled in specialised areas. You can ask the counsellor about their most recent continued professional development to ensure that they are keeping up with standards and professional development. All counsellors are responsible for ensuring continued professional development. Maintaining this development helps them stay up to date with the latest professional standards. It enhances their knowledge and ensures they remain up to speed in modern approaches.

Records.

Counsellors must keep session records, both session/clinical notes and process notes. Session/clinical notes relate to the client and are used as an aid memoire. They should be factual, clear, accurate and concise and contain information about what the client discussed in the sessions. The counsellor's personal opinions should not be included. Counselling clients have the right to request to see these notes if they wish to.

Process notes are written by the counsellor for their supervision sessions. They should focus on the interaction between the counsellor and the supervisor. They would relate to the counsellor's thoughts and feelings about their work and any issues they wish to discuss. Keeping good client records is crucial for professional practice. It is very important to maintain these records in the event of any complaint or claim. A judge will state that counselling did not happen if there are no counselling records offered. You must always be informed by the counsellor that written records from the counselling sessions will be kept. As part of the session notes, all communications with clients should be documented in them. Client records must be retained for a minimum of seven years, after which they may be securely destroyed, typically by shredding. Records relating to children and young people should be kept for a longer period, in accordance with legal and professional guidelines. Records must be stored in a confidential and secure manner. For example, paper records should be locked in secure storage, while digital records should be password-protected, encrypted, and backed up on a flash drive. Maintaining accurate records is crucial in delivering effective client care. Client records are a significant aspect of the counselling process. They help counsellors to comply with legal regulations, track client progress, and ensure continuous care.

Private practice.

Private practice means managing finances, a suitable office space, legal issues, insurance, marketing, contracts, notes, the General Data Protection Regulation, a website, fees, and much more. A small number are not sufficiently qualified but are offering online counselling services. It would be in your interest to find out all about your counsellor before you book any sessions, whether it is private practice, online or with a counselling organisation. Ensure that the counsellor is qualified and working professionally. It is important for you to ask the counsellor questions on these important aspects -

- ➢ What professional body are you registered with?
- ➢ What are your qualifications?
- ➢ Do you follow an ethical code?
- ➢ Can you explain confidentiality?
- ➢ Do you have regular supervision?
- ➢ How do you keep my information safe?
- ➢ Are you insured?

Ethical Accountability.

Counsellors are responsible for their actions and accountable for the services that they provide. They must be open about mishaps and let clients know if something has gone wrong. For example, breaching boundaries or causing emotional distress. They must make informed decisions when faced with complex issues.

Ethical responsibility and accountability are of the utmost importance in counselling. It is the foundation of the profession and means that clients are protected and counsellors preserve principles and honesty. If counsellors are not acting in an ethical manner, then it affects clients, themselves and the profession. Ethical guidelines ensure that clients receive excellent care. They regulate the practice and behaviour of counsellors, including confidentiality, client autonomy, client welfare and help them to handle complex aspects of their work.

Chapter Ten

Counselling Helpful Or Harmful

Double edged sword

The right words can be empowering, while the wrong ones can be negative and damaging.

Challenges in mental health have increased in our often stressful and fast-moving world, and many people are seeking help from counselling. Whilst counselling can be very helpful to many people, it does not always help everyone and cannot resolve all issues. When it is offered by a competent counsellor, it is more likely to be helpful than harmful. It can be harmful if it is not provided appropriately for the client's needs.

Helpful Counselling.

Counselling can offer emotional support to help clients' well-being. It can improve self-awareness and manage many client issues. It can help with communication skills and relationships, self-esteem, and managing stress, anxiety, and depression. Coping with life's challenges is not always easy, and counselling can be helpful and productive. Counsellors empower clients to help with confidence, self-acceptance and assist clients through their challenges. Counselling can be incredibly beneficial; however, its success may be different for each individual person. It can be helpful for most clients, as long as it is fitted to the needs of each individual client.

Further benefits of counselling include helping clients to understand the issues that they bring by offering support and helping clients to manage their emotional distress. Client issues and experiences can be shared safely with a counsellor in a confidential space. One of the most important aspects of counselling is the therapeutic relationship between counsellor and client. A good relationship ensures that clients do not feel uncomfortable when discussing their issues. Rapport and trust develop the relationship together with a feeling that the counsellor is genuine, empathic and understanding. Many clients state that they feel heard for the first time, and some state that they have made important life changes through counselling.

Counselling certainly can be beneficial by improving mental well-being. It can help to reduce stress and help with confusion and feeling overwhelmed, it can enable insight and self-awareness. Counselling can be effective and beneficial, and help many people to improve their mental health.

Harmful Counselling.

Counselling can be extremely helpful, but it has limitations. There are risks if it is not applied appropriately. Counselling cannot help clients with issues that relate to finances, legal concerns or physical illnesses. It may not produce the desired outcome for some clients. There are considerable differences in counsellors and variability in outcomes. Successful outcomes have more to do with the counsellor and their experience and competence than anything else.

Counselling may cause harm if there is not a good match with the counsellor. It could be miscommunication, an unsuitable therapeutic approach, or the counsellor may be inexperienced. A counsellor's personal or cultural beliefs may lessen the benefits of the counselling. Unfortunately, there is very little research on the harmful effects of counselling and even less on evaluating counsellors. Negative and harmful experiences with counsellors have increased over a period of time. But recognising a poor counsellor or bad counselling can be quite difficult. A bad counsellor may offer ineffective interventions or the wrong therapeutic approach. Both of these will prevent any progression. A counsellor who does not appreciate difference and diversity can cause harm.

Effects of harmful counselling on clients.

Harm and abuse of any kind in counselling can have huge psychological, physical, and emotional effects on clients. It may leave you feeling confused and unable to trust. Do not take on any blame as it is the counsellor who is at fault. If you ever feel that a counsellor is abusing you in any way, it is essential to end the counselling and report the abuse. Counsellor abuse is a serious issue within the counselling profession. Counselling, in some cases, can cause anxiety for clients, even depression. This may be when a counsellor uses dubious techniques. Bad counsellors may be incompetent or may take advantage of clients. Some will breach boundaries or have poor concentration. Bad counsellors risk causing harm to clients; they may weaken trust and cause emotional upset.

Personal Reflection.

Counselling can often be a difficult experience for some clients. *I know of a good friend of mine who had counselling on two occasions. The first was cognitive behavioural therapy. My friend attended four times and was given 'homework', which was worksheets to complete. Each of the occasions my friend saw the counsellor, the session time was greatly reduced. In that last session, the counsellor didn't even look over the worksheets, and my friend stopped attending. It would appear that the counsellor and counselling were ineffective. My friend, some months later, went to see a counsellor connected to a doctor's surgery, and this* *was person-centred counselling. My friend left this counselling after just three sessions. Apparently, the counsellor hardly spoke and offered few questions and little feedback. My friend will never have counselling again due to the incompetence of these counsellors.*

Another friend used the national health services for online counselling. They did all the online work over a period of time and spoke with a counsellor on several occasions. It helped my friend considerably, and I would use the service again if they needed to. Since becoming a counsellor, I have had counselling on two separate occasions. The first was person-centred counselling and the second was integrative counselling. I had six sessions the first time and 10 sessions the second time. I took a different concern with each one. They were both really helpful.

Financial Exploitation.

Financial exploitation in any form is unacceptable. Counselling is a very private interaction with clients, bringing their issues of distress and emotional turmoil and sharing personal and intimate details about themselves. Some clients may be extremely vulnerable and are easy pickings for a greedy counsellor. Power and manipulation play a large part in financial abuse. It can cause emotional damage as well as financial loss. This abuse is mainly found in the private sector and may be as simple as a counsellor increasing their fees or charging for sessions that did not occur, or it could be recommending that clients have more counselling sessions. The counsellor will wait for a good relationship and trust to have developed, especially with vulnerable clients.

Sexual Abuse.

Sexual abuse is completely inappropriate. It may be sexual talking and flirting or improper touching, all of which may lead to a physical relationship. This kind of abuse is all about power and dominance. It happens more often than you may imagine. The relationship between client and counsellor is an intimate one, but this is a therapeutic intimacy where the counsellor must maintain a professional, psychological and therapeutic distance. Any type of sexual attention is not acceptable and ultimately destroys the relationship. Awareness of a sexual attraction is one thing, but acting upon it is unethical and damaging. Any sexual attention is against the code of conduct. A red flag will be if the counsellor frequently addresses issues of a sexual nature. You must end the relationship and report the counsellor.

Incompetent counsellors.

Incompetent counsellors fail to observe the standards required. They cross boundaries, may be judgmental towards you or prejudiced in terms of your race, sexuality or ethnicity. They lack the skills required of a proficient counsellor, which makes their counselling ineffective. Ensure that you have a counsellor who offers you the professional and effective counselling that you are entitled to.

Personal Reflection.

When I was a supervisor for an organisation working with clients who had experienced sexual abuse and/or domestic violence, *I supervised some very professional counsellors, and I recall three in particular who were an absolute pleasure to work with. They were caring, empathic, and skilled. However, others within the organisation, including both qualified and trainee counsellors, were mediocre or simply incompetent. Several should not have been working as counsellors, especially not with the complex issues surrounding sexual abuse and domestic violence. A number of very vulnerable clients were not receiving the caring, respectful, and professional help they deserved. I explained some critical concerns to these counsellors and tried, on* *more than one occasion, to support them in improving their practice. Unfortunately, nothing seemed to change.*

I spoke to the manager several times and also raised these issues with the trustees during an organised meeting, but my concerns went unheard. I could not condone the continued ineffectiveness of certain counsellors, nor the poor support and inadequate counselling that clients were receiving. I had no alternative but to leave the organisation.

It is unfortunate that many instances of client abuse are never reported, mainly due to the difficulty in proving that they happened. Counselling must be, by its very nature, private, involving only the counsellor and the client, and without recorded sessions, there is often no evidence to confirm claims of abuse. It is not easy for clients to recognise abuse, accepting it as part of the counselling process. Ongoing abuse can leave clients feeling distressed and confused.

Incompetent and harmful counsellors are in the minority, but they continue to practice, whilst lacking empathy, respect and encouragement. They may be dismissive and unprofessional. They could be defensive and resistant. Their counselling will not offer any progress and could cause harm. Good counsellors will enable you to feel respected, empowered, heard and understood. It is important to find a qualified, ethical, and experienced professional counsellor who offers a safe and supportive environment. Finding the right counsellor is crucial. They must be professional, qualified, experienced, and belong to a professional counselling body.

Counsellors have a responsibility to both their profession and their client work. Their ethical practice will offer trust and commitment. They must also act in the client's best interest and take responsibility for their actions. Competent counsellors will provide effective, ethical care. They will continue to have ongoing professional development. Counsellors are accountable to their professional body as well as to their clients. They must maintain clarity in all aspects of the counselling process.

Counselling is strongly considered helpful, but it is not without risks or limitations. Though infrequent, harm can occur, especially when the counselling is not matched to the client. It can be a helpful experience when it is done ethically and with the right counsellor. Counselling can be life-changing, but if boundaries are crossed or ethics are ignored, it can also cause harm.

Chapter Eleven

Client Rights And Counsellor Wrongs

'Sounds of neglect, broken trust, quiet whispers'

Client Rights.

As a counselling client, you have a number of rights. I feel it is only fair and appropriate that you should be aware of these rights. Also, knowing what your rights are will enable you to determine whether or not your counsellor is working with you professionally and ethically. You must feel sufficiently reassured to discuss your rights. The following list is not exhaustive, but it will enable you to consider some of what you are entitled to.

When choosing a counsellor –

Ensure the counsellor will meet your requirements, will give you details about their qualifications and experience and a copy of their code of ethics.

Will give you, in writing, exactly what is being offered, e.g., times, fees, how to pay, number of sessions available, etc.

Will answer your questions to include the type of counselling theory, the techniques and approaches they use.

Make you aware that you can end the counselling at any time.

Will give you all the documentation, as described in previous chapters, relating to commencing counselling.

During counselling-

- You have the right to expect dignity and respect and consideration and not to be discriminated against for any reason.

- You have the right to feel safe, relaxed and comfortable during your counselling sessions.
- You have the right to ethical treatment. This means that the counsellor should abide by a set of values, act in a principled manner and adhere to the ethical framework.
- You have the right to confidentiality. Anything that you say in the counselling sessions is confidential and should remain so, with some exceptions. The counsellor can breach this confidentiality if they suspect that you may harm yourself or others, or anything that is related to sexual abuse, historical or current.
- You have the right to access your records at any time
- You have the right to receive counselling that respects individual differences.
- You have the right to make a complaint in confidence.
- You have the right to check on the progress of the sessions. This should be done by the counsellor periodically, and if this is not done, then you must request a discussion on your general progress.
- You have the right to be informed about the boundaries involved in the therapeutic relationship.
- You are entitled to information regarding your rights, and counsellors are obliged to make sure that your rights are being met. If your counsellor is not acknowledging your client's rights, then they are not working professionally and, as most codes of ethics for counsellors contain a section on client rights, they are also not working ethically.
- You need to expect a level of empathy and understanding from their counsellors, compassion and support and certainly confidentiality.

- Counsellors must be professional and offer each client an individual approach that includes empowerment.
- If your needs are not being met, then there will be little progress and a lack of trust; overall, it will negatively affect your self-esteem and have an impact on your mental health.
- Ensure you feel safe, comfortable, have trust in the counsellor and feel heard and understood.
- If you feel uncomfortable, unhappy or pressured by the counsellor or that the counsellor has been abusive in any way, then you must act upon your feelings and trust your instinct. If something feels wrong, then it generally is wrong. Stop the sessions and make a complaint.

Counsellor Wrongs.

Counselling is dependent on clients putting their trust in counsellors, and this trust will develop good standards of care. Counsellors have a specific duty of care to you, which includes safety, both physical and psychological, and treating you respectfully. Counsellors should not be judgmental or discriminatory. They should not ignore your concerns or end sessions prematurely. They must abide by the ethical codes of practice and not distance themselves from the code.

Counsellors who fail to meet the ethical standards should not practice as they will cause upset and distress to clients.

Monitoring and Reflecting.

It is unethical for counsellors not to monitor and reflect on their work, as this is an essential aspect of professional practice. The assessment of client sessions, including the impact of the session on themselves is important. Assessments can be formal or informal and must be done on a regular basis. Evaluate what went well and what was not effective in the progress and the outcome. It can offer focus and structure, and can enhance reflection and improve the relationship.

It is wrong for counsellors not to monitor and reflect on their practice, as they will not be acting ethically or professionally.

Commitment.

Commitment is most important for productive client care. A lack of commitment may cause the counselling to be ineffective. Being committed to clients and their counselling is based on ethical principles, which are important for sustaining trust and providing good counselling practices. Commitment is about counsellors observing the competence and integrity of the counselling profession.

It is wrong and unethical for counsellors who are not committed to practice.

Referrals.

Counsellors must always be aware of their personal and professional limitations and levels of competence. They should recognise their own vulnerabilities, especially when working with clients who push them outside their comfort zone. They must acknowledge when they are not able to work adequately with clients. In these cases, a handover should be discussed openly and professionally, and the client referred to another professional. It is wrong for a counsellor to continue working with a client once they are aware of their own limitations. A different type of counsellor or additional services may be more appropriate.

In these cases, it would be highly inappropriate for a counsellor to continue working with the client, knowing their lack of competence or limitations.

Crisis and Risk.

Counsellors may sometimes experience challenging times; they have an obligation to act. It may be breaching confidentiality, assessing risks or safeguarding measures for cases such as suicidal ideation, or child protection concerns. It is unacceptable to ignore a crisis or risk.

Confidentiality must be maintained as far as possible, but it may be breached when necessary. Such instances must be reported to the relevant services, and all actions must be properly documented. These steps are essential for ethical and legal compliance within the counselling profession.

Failure to act or acting inappropriately is both unethical and unacceptable.

Boundaries.

An important aspect of the ethical framework is boundaries, which form the basis of counselling contracts and sessions. They create a safe and supportive space for clients. When boundaries are breached, trust in the relationship is lost. Boundaries protect clients from harm and poor counselling.

Examples of boundary breaches are dual relationships, meaning counsellors cannot counsel a friend, relative, colleague or neighbour. They should not form a friendship with a client outside of counselling sessions. Counsellors must not begin sessions late or end sessions early. It is wrong for counsellors not to be aware of cultural differences. It is preferable for counsellors not to touch clients during counselling sessions. The role of touch in counselling is complex and sometimes problematic.

One of the most important aspects of boundaries is confidentiality. Counsellors must always explain this to clients. They must also know when to break confidentiality. This is usually for risks of harm, for example, a client who has suicidal thoughts or intentions, where the counsellor must follow the appropriate policies. There are also legal limitations, such as acts of terrorism, money laundering or drug trafficking. The counsellor is obliged to pass the information onto the police, and client notes will be requested by a judge. Risk of harm to others is normally about protecting children and vulnerable adults, which is a safeguarding issue, and confidentiality will have to be broken. There are also issues of sexual abuse and historical sexual abuse that come under maintaining or breaking confidentiality.

Personal Reflection.

There are some counsellors who may hold a client's hand or offer them a hug, and, in some respects, this may be of value to the client, but it can also be misinterpreted. *I shake a client's hand, but no more than that, as I consider the relationship a professional one. Taking touch, any further may damage the counselling relationship. Counsellors must remember that it is a therapeutic relationship where psychological distance must be maintained for the benefit of the client and the counselling. While some argue that touch has therapeutic value, its misuse can lead to harm, making it a sensitive issue in counselling. I have discussed this issue many times with trainee counsellors, supervisors and colleagues with many differing opinions.*

Respecting these boundaries is the counsellor's obligation, and they should not be breached. In very few circumstances, some boundaries may be stretched a little, but this should never happen without the counsellor first discussing the situation in supervision or if it is genuinely in a client's interest.

Personal Reflection.

Boundaries have their role in counselling; however, there is sometimes a lack of clarity regarding breaches. *Reports of boundary* *breaches are often overlooked, leading to inadequate accountability, with many complaints remaining confidential. Breaches of boundaries will cause clients to lose trust in the counsellor. I have been aware of counsellors breaching boundaries on a few occasions. One breach was making friends with a client and meeting with them between sessions. It came to light when a colleague of mine had seen them together a couple of times. The breach was reported, and the counsellor was reprimanded, and an action plan was put in force by her supervisor. A second breach was one of the worst, a breach of confidentiality. This counsellor had shared a client's details and their issues with two colleagues. One of the colleagues had guessed who the client was and had reported the counsellor. The counsellor belonged to a professional body, and they lost their position at the counselling organisation.*

Malpractice.

Malpractice is any form of negligence by a counsellor. It means that a counsellor is not working ethically or professionally and is breaching their obligation of care. They are failing to meet their professional standards. Counsellors must have well-defined boundaries and understand their duty of care, as there will be consequences for breaching this.

Any form of malpractice is wrong and causes harm to clients.

Competence.

Counsellor competence is difficult to recognise. Competence is the ability to make good judgments. An incompetent counsellor will lack empathy and perhaps even encourage dependence. These counsellors can cause harm to clients. A counsellor's competence involves their knowledge of skills, theories and understanding. Counsellors who are incompetent may be judgmental or use critical language; they may not listen to you or look at you.

Such counsellors are contravening the code of ethics. Assessing competence when it is put into practice with clients is impossible, as the client and counsellor are together with no third party to do any assessing. Incompetence is wrong and should never be accepted.

Personal Reflection.

I recollect a client who discussed childhood sexual abuse with their male counsellor. *The counsellor decided to hug the client at the end of the session. The client was naturally confused and upset as the hug from a man brought back unpleasant memories; she did not continue the counselling. I knew of a trainee counsellor who was working way beyond her capabilities with a young person and ended up with a very distressed client. The client's mother phoned the organisation to talk to the counsellor and discuss her daughter's distress. The phone call was put through to the counsellor instead of the manager, and the counsellor shared everything about the client with her mother. This was a breach of confidentiality and unethical. The situation ended with the trainee being told to leave the placement and taken off the course. Just a few examples of counsellor incompetence.*

Only a small percentage of counsellors move outside their ethical guidelines. Most professionals are committed to helping you heal and grow. However, as the number of counsellors increases, so may the number of those who do not practise responsibly. You deserve to feel safe and respected in counselling. If you ever feel uneasy with your counsellor, or if your sessions are not helping you to move forward, it is acceptable to end the sessions and raise your concerns. Your emotional well-being comes first, and making a complaint will empower you.

Counsellors must always act in the client's best interests and take responsibility for their actions. Competent counsellors should offer effective, ethical and informed support. Which should also include ethical maturity, reflective practice and cultural competence.

Counsellors must always observe the boundaries, which are an important aspect of the ethical framework. They ensure safety, clarity and professionalism. They protect both the client and the counsellor, they prevent ethical breaches and emotional involvement, and they promote trust and coherence in the therapeutic process.

Chapter Twelve

Integrating Technology Into Counselling Practice

Preserving Human Connection in a Digital Counselling World

'Technology enables us to connect with anyone, anywhere, but it cannot tell us what to say. It can give us power, but it cannot tell us how to use it.'

Since the COVID19 pandemic, the integration of technology into counselling practice has expanded significantly. Digital platforms have enabled individuals experiencing mental health difficulties to access therapeutic support remotely, whether through online services or telephonebased interventions. In the postpandemic period, a wide range of online resources for counsellors has emerged, contributing to the increased costeffectiveness and accessibility of remote counselling. Furthermore, technology now plays a more prominent role in counsellor training and supervision, supporting the development of professional competence in contemporary practice.

Technology is offering clients many different ways of accessing counselling. It has enabled choices for communicating without the need to travel and a better range of options for appointments. It is essential to consider that technology should not replace the human connection of face-to-face counselling. Whilst technology is gaining popularity in counselling, be aware that there are some limitations in the different methods used.

Communication methods.

Phone counselling – used by clients who do not or cannot access technology or who are not comfortable with face-to-face counselling sessions. It is good for clients who are not proficient in computers or who have poor internet connections. It is also useful for clients who do not wish to be seen. Clients who wish to use phone counselling require a comfortable and quiet place to be able to communicate their emotional issues.

Pros

Geographical location enables sessions with no need for travelling. It is convenient and useful for clients with physical disabilities or social phobias. The counselling is audio only, and the counsellor cannot observe your body language and can only take signs from the tone of your voice. You may be asked frequently to share your feelings.

Cons The counselling is audio only and the counsellor cannot observe your body language and can only take signs from the tone of your voice You may be asked frequently to share your feelings.

Video counselling – This appears to be the most popular and the closest to face-to-face counselling. It is a real-time, face-to-face interaction which enables a reasonably good therapeutic relationship. Clients may feel more relaxed in the comfort and privacy of their own homes. It is almost as effective as face-to-face counselling, but not quite. Clients will need a good internet connection, and security is paramount.

Pros

It is accessible, especially for anyone living in distant areas. More affordable than face-to-face counselling. Sessions can be flexible.

Cons

There may be issues with technology, such as a poor internet connection. Also, privacy issues, i.e. security or disruptions in the home.

Messaging – text communication is for clients who may prefer not to be seen or heard, wishing to be anonymous. Clients who want to take their time when communicating. Messaging is an instantaneous conversation, either using an agreed time with the counsellor or clients sending messages in their own time, and counsellors responding when it is convenient for them. Both client and counsellor will have a written record of the counselling interactions. There may be instances when there is cause for misunderstanding. It is not such a popular method.

Pros

Accessibility, communicating with the counsellor at any given time, wherever you are. Anonymity and time for reflection. Lower cost than face-to-face counselling.

Cons

Responses can be delayed. The possibility of misinterpretation may occur with no verbal or audio cues. Extra work for the counsellor when responding to difficult issues or situations.

Email – clients who prefer to communicate over a longer period of time and who like to convey in writing. It is useful for clients who have busy lifestyles, who may find it difficult to arrange appointment times. Clients may feel uncomfortable when disclosing personal information in a face-to-face session. Clients and counsellors are able to offer more informed and reasoned responses. Both client and counsellor will have a written record of the counselling interactions. Again, not such a popular method.

Pros

Flexibility, writing whenever it suits you. Time for reflection. Accessible, especially if you have physical disabilities.

Cons.

The lack of non-verbal and audio cues limits the interaction in terms of the counsellor being unable to appreciate the client's reaction and emotions. Feedback is not always immediate. Possible misunderstandings due to a lack of verbal and audio cues.

Each method of communication has its own advantages and disadvantages; however, they all offer accessibility and flexibility. Technology is giving clients a greater choice of how they would like to access counselling. It can also remove barriers and is beneficial to both clients and counsellors through improved accessibility and increased privacy.

Pros and Cons of Technology in Counselling

Pros

- ➢ Convenience, accessibility and flexible session times.
- ➢ Anonymity and your own familiar environment.
- ➢ Therapeutic tools such as mood tracking and journaling.
- ➢ Chat services for crisis support.

Cons

- ➢ The loss of the human connection
- ➢ Reduced non-verbal cues.

- ➢ Security and privacy risks.
- ➢ Confidentiality concerns.
- ➢ Older clients are unable to use or access technology.
- ➢ Overreliance on technology.

Ethical Issues.

There are a number of ethical issues connected to technology in counselling. Although it is accessible and convenient, there are also concerns and challenges. Counsellors must understand the responsibility that comes with technology.

Data – A client's data must never be misused and must be kept completely private and confidential. Care must be taken in respect of unlawful access or data breaches.

Informed Consent – clients need to be aware of how their data will be used and stored. They must also be made aware of the details and complexities of the technology used.

Security/privacy – All counselling sessions using technology must be secure. To include secure storage and encrypted systems. There may be a risk of breaches, and sensitive data is at risk from hacking.

Counsellor Competence – It is important that counsellors are well-trained to use the technology and able to fix issues when they arise connected with technology. Ethical guidelines are really important in making sure that counsellors are knowledgeable and proficient.

Technical issues – There may be faults with software and difficulties with connections. They may disturb sessions and will have a negative effect on the counselling process.

Emergencies – Clear procedures must be followed for emergency situations. It is impossible to provide instant help for a client using a phone or video call.

Cultural understanding and availability – Technology needs to be accessible to all clients and all backgrounds. Different clients will have differing amounts of expertise with technology.

All ethical recommendations need to be available to counsellors and followed by them.

Regulations need to be complied with. The use of technology in counselling requires high standards of practice.

Online or in person?

A decision that only you can make. This must be based upon your personal choice and circumstances, which you prefer, and what is best for you. What makes you feel supported and most comfortable? The conventional method of counselling has always been face-to-face, with most counsellors being trained in this method. However, times have changed and continue to do so. Technology is now part of counselling.

Things to consider when choosing the right method for yourself: Do you want - Rapport and Relationship Building, Safety, Security and Confidentiality, Accessibility and Convenience or Availability and Flexibility?

The benefits of both methods are similar; consider the pros and cons of each one.

In Person.

A counsellor can read non-verbal cues, which helps with understanding your feelings and emotions. The room is secure and private. The counsellor can offer support. However, the counselling may be more expensive than online counselling.

Online.

Can take place wherever you are, as long as it is secure and private for you. It may cost less than in face-to-face counselling. There may be difficulties with technology and privacy, and security concerns.

Some counsellors are already using a hybrid model and, no doubt, many more will follow suit. A hybrid model means that the counsellor will use a combination of online and face-to-face sessions to suit your availability. It is a good, versatile approach that is useful for differing requirements and choices. It allows clients and counsellors to choose the most suitable format based on needs and circumstances.

The Future of Counselling with Technology.

Many counsellors have welcomed technology, whilst others are not so sure and do not want technology to completely take over. Counselling's future is being changed by technology, and as it continues to progress, clients may be introduced to many different technological methods to help them. It is important to appreciate that there are a number of people who cannot or do not use technology and who will need to rely on face-to-face counselling.

There are already computer programs for Cognitive Behaviour Therapy. Also, artificial intelligence-powered chatbots, which have become more advanced, offer guidance, psychoeducation and support. Virtual reality is now being used, simulating true-to-life experiences which can be used for anxiety, phobias and post-traumatic stress disorder. Wearable technology and digital tools used for assessing client moods, feelings and anxiety are also in use. These are the future, but they are not able to offer empathy, trust or understanding, intuition or emotions. They are unable to read non-verbal cues or be aware of cultural sensitivities, and are not able to help with complex or severe mental health issues.

Personal Reflection.

My own experience of using technology in counselling has been reasonable. *For many years, I have worked face-to-face, and I personally feel that the experience for clients is so much better than through the use of technology. However, I realised the impact that it had on both clients and counsellors, especially during the COVID-19 pandemic. I appreciate how much more accessible, flexible and convenient it is for a number of clients, whether that is phone counselling or video counselling. In the main, it is also more affordable.*

My reservations are concerned with counsellor training. More and more of this training is being offered online with little opportunity to practice face to face with fellow trainees and to relate to others, sharing experiences, asking questions and assisting each other. I worry that the use of technology will further dilute counsellor training generally. I am also disturbed about the amount of supervision that takes place online. For qualified counsellors, I can accept this, but for trainee counsellors, I feel face-to-face supervision throughout their training would be far more beneficial.

Whatever my feelings about technology in counselling, counsellor training and supervision, I appreciate that it is the future and will continue to be used. Some say that it is transforming counselling, whilst others are not so sure.

When it is used ethically, technology can enhance counselling, but it should never be allowed to replace it. It is essential to consider the benefits and the limitations of using technology. The development of standards of efficiency for counsellors is crucial; a range of skills, understanding and knowledge is required. Counsellors must work safely and ethically.

Whether technology is welcomed or resisted, it has become a permanent fixture in counselling and in many people's everyday lives. It is gaining momentum and is opening up new possibilities, and it cannot be reversed. However, it brings challenges along with it, such as privacy issues, ethics and confidentiality. Vigilance is needed to make sure that safety, standards and the human interaction remain. Gaining trust, presence and empathy are difficult to consolidate on a screen.

In the end, the most effective counselling does not come from accessing technology, but from the strength of understanding between the counsellor and client. Love it or loathe it, it is here to stay.

Chapter Thirteen

Evaluating The Need For Change

Reimagining Counselling: Where Do We Go from Here?

'Echoes of development and change are what matter now'

Counselling is often portrayed as a compassionate and supportive endeavour; however, there exist many complexities which reveal that change across several areas is required. The profession generally upholds ethical standards, but instances of malpractice, breaches of conduct, and counsellors' weaknesses continue to emerge.

Over the last few years, the use of technology in counselling has increased. Whilst face-to-face counselling continues to be used, online counselling has become much more popular. With this increase in technology comes a small but gradual decline in the quality of many other aspects of the profession. In particular, the integrity and professionalism of some counsellors. I would never criticise the counselling profession, but simply wish to highlight areas that need care and accountability. Change is required through openness, responsibility and quality.

Professional Bodies.

It would be beneficial for counselling professional bodies to begin to work together, share insights, learn from each other and recognise similarities. They could work more with their members, as discussions could increase development. Complaints procedures could be upgraded, and strengthening regulation and accreditation processes would be helpful for maintaining high standards of counsellors. Professional bodies need to offer more essential assistance to their members.

Awarding Bodies.

Awarding bodies need to be more responsible for counselling qualifications, raising standards for counselling portfolios. Regular curriculum updates are needed, together with technology training. Higher standards should be set; further guidance should be provided, and development improved. Awarding and Professional bodies have a huge influence on the counselling profession; they need to change with the times, to modify and develop.

Counsellor Training Centres.

The current counselling training centres need to shape up. There should be further understanding of how to train counsellors. Trainers need to have teaching qualifications and experience. They should be proficient counsellors and fully understand the course qualifications. Assignments should be above average, and internally assessed work should be marked more objectively. Cultural and social differences and underrepresented minorities are not always included in the curriculum. Inclusivity and diversity need to be taught. New theoretical approaches should be discussed, and the centres should have extensive information in the form of books and journals, as well as useful and functional practical ways of working. Training in technology is needed as well as neurodiversity and cultural competence.

Trainee counsellor placements need to be more selective when taking on trainee counsellors and must ensure that they have an induction, a mentor and several months of monitoring. They should be given clients to work with who have been assessed and who do not have complex issues or have been diagnosed with challenging mental health issues. A large percentage of trainee counsellors beginning their placements may not be able to give clients what they need. Many just do not have what it takes to become counsellors.

Trainers.

Counselling trainers should remain updated on research, counselling theories and techniques. Their ongoing counselling will strengthen the trainee sessions. Training should never lack interest, be tedious or outdated. Trainers need to be highly motivated, offer new techniques, demonstrations and much more practice for trainees; more creative and innovative approaches should be used to prepare counsellors to offer high-quality counselling. The trainers need to be well-qualified counsellors with teaching qualifications. They should be well-versed in the curriculum and able to offer trainees a professionally taught course.

Regulation.

One of the main aspects that necessitates change is the Government Statutory Registration of counsellors. This would begin to guarantee that counsellors with good qualifications, skills and expertise are safe to practice. The statutory registration of counsellors is a decision that the United Kingdom Government should make, and for at least the past two decades, it has decided against it. At the time of writing, nothing has happened. Without statutory legislation, vulnerable clients are being harmed.

Theoretical Approaches.

The theoretical approaches introduced over the years are still being used effectively in counselling. More recently, many other approaches have been introduced; some are particularly useful, whilst others are unconventional. Training counsellors in some of the newer theoretical approaches is necessary to guarantee that their theories are not misinterpreted or badly carried out. Some new approaches can be combined with traditional approaches to help clients with their specific issues.

Employers.

The demand for counsellors has grown considerably; however, for the number of counsellors who qualify, there is not the same number of counselling jobs on offer. Most employers of counsellors will look for those who have a large amount of client work experience and additional counselling-related qualifications. It is recommended that newly qualified counsellors should take further training to build on their knowledge and continue with professional development. Further courses are offered by some centres to enhance counsellor skills to help them find employment.

Lawsuits.

Complaints and lawsuits have recently been on the increase as the demand for mental health services escalates. You must choose your counsellor carefully, check their qualifications, experience and accreditation, take your time, ask your questions, feel comfortable with the counsellor and trust your instincts.

Lawsuits involve unethical conduct, harm caused through incompetence, boundary breaches and failure to maintain professional standards. To reduce complaints and misconduct warrants much stronger regulatory systems. Clients must come first and should be the primary focus for counsellors throughout all counselling sessions. For those counsellors who cause harm, there would most likely be disciplinary action. Without statutory regulation, many counsellors who are unethical may avoid consequences.

Standards.

Standards in counselling are of considerable importance and should be regularly assessed. New forms of training are required; new procedures and strategies are needed to check counsellors' and supervisors' abilities. Raising standards should be a common goal for awarding and professional bodies. Newly qualified counsellors require more help and support systems to ensure they can provide effective care. Many have limited experience and would find it difficult to work with complex cases effectively. They need ongoing training and supervision support to increase their confidence and ability to practice. Acknowledging counselling's limitations is essential for creating a more transparent and accountable practice. By engaging constructively with both its strengths and its weaknesses, professionals can contribute to the evolution of counselling into a truly strong and reputable profession.

Counselling needs to change, to make it more accessible, effective, and fair. Hundreds of people are waiting for mental health support; changes must prioritize mental health waiting lists. The increase of online counselling is a concern in terms of vulnerable clients being left behind. Also, early intervention hubs, particularly for young people, need to be prioritised. There should be counsellors available in all schools.

The future of counselling is about adapting to change. Inclusivity is paramount, it is crucial that diversity and difference are respected, inclusion means that every voice should be heard, valued, and empowered.

Whilst the counselling profession upholds ethical standards, there are aspects left unaddressed. I have attempted to offer a balanced perspective through insight and understanding, in addition, shedding light on areas of counselling that require change. Meeting client needs and improving client care require change, accountability and progress are required. While the profession may face some challenges, counselling remains really important and you deserve the high-quality care that most counsellors offer.

The aim of this book has been to provide you with a deeper understanding of counselling, what it is and how it works. With greater knowledge you are in a better place to decide whether counselling is right for you, what to look for in a counsellor, and how counselling works. My goal has also been to offer aspects of the profession that are often hidden, not to discourage you, but to enable you to be perceptive so that you are equipped to make informed and wise choices.

Counselling Resources

There are a lot of charities, community services and helplines available for anyone struggling with mental health issues. Ask at Citizens Advice, your GP surgery or your local Council for the names of helplines, support groups and online communities.

Below are lists of helpful free services.

SUPPORT AND HELPLINES

ENGLAND

Mind Helpline – offering support and guidance. Call 0300 102 1234 Monday to Friday 9am to 6pm. Samaritans – 24/7 free helpline at 116 123 of Hope – online directory for free mental health charities.

Mental Health Matters – provides regional services in England.

SCOTLAND

National Health Service - 24 Mental Health Hub – Call 111 and select the mental health option for free 24/7 support.

Breathing Space – Free confidential phone/webchat service for anyone aged 16+ feeling distressed. Call 0800 83 85 87.

Scottish Action for Mental Health - Offers walk-in hubs ("The Nook") and community services.

Togetherall – Free online peer-support community available via participating councils.

Citizens Advice Scotland – Guidance on accessing NHS and community mental health services.

WALES

National Health Service Wales, (option 2) – Free urgent mental health support, available 24/7.

Mind Cymru – Local branches offering free mental health support across Wales.

C.A.L.L. Helpline (Advice and listening line) – 24/7 confidential support. Call 0800 132 737.

Public Health Wales– Provides information and access to free wellbeing support.

Crwsh– Online resource listing mental wellbeing services.

IE IRELAND

HSE Mental health services– Free services via GP referral, local mental health units, or hospitals.

Samaritans Ireland– Free 24/7 helpline at 116 123.

Text About It (50808) – Free 24/7 text support. Text HELLO to 50808.

Mental Health Ireland– Provides information and links to free support.

Mental health matters– Directory of support services nationwide.

SELF-CARE PLAN

A self-care plan can help you stay grounded and emotionally well, especially if you are

waiting for counselling or are currently having counselling. This will enable mental and emotional well-being.

You might find it helpful to write down your thoughts, feelings, or questions as they arise. Mindfulness or gentle meditation can support emotional steadiness. If you like using digital tools, apps such as Headspace or Calm offer guided practices. If you are preparing for counselling, make notes about what you hope to explore and how you are feeling. If you are already in counselling, take a moment after each session to reflect on any insights or themes.

Keep in touch with people who feel safe and supportive. Reach out to trusted friends or family when you need connection. Listen to music that soothes or uplifts you. Stay active in ways that feel manageable for your body. Eat regularly, choose nourishing foods, and drink enough water. Use simple breathing exercises to help calm your system. Make time for rest and relaxation, even in small moments. Try to maintain a sleep routine that helps you unwind. Move at a pace that feels right for you. Gently bring your attention back to the present when your mind wanders.

APPS AND DIGITAL TOOLS

Headspace and Calm offer guided meditations, breathing exercises, and sleep support.

Daylio and Reflectly help you track your mood, habits, and reflections.

Strides can support gentle goalsetting and progress tracking.

Pzizz offers help with rest and naps.

Sleep Cycle provides insight into your sleep patterns. These tools can complement counselling by helping you build awareness and consistency.

GROUNDING AND RELAXATION TECHNIQUES

54321 Grounding:

Notice five things you can see. Notice four things you can touch.

Notice three things you can hear. Notice two things you can smell.

Notice one thing you can taste.

This exercise helps bring your attention back to the present moment.

PROGRESSIVE MUSCLE RELAXATION

Sit or lie down in a comfortable position and close your eyes if that feels comfortable. Take a slow breath in and let it go. Move through your body one area at a time. For each group of muscles, tighten gently, hold for a few seconds, then release and notice the softening.

Hands and arms: Clench your fists, hold, and release. Notice the warmth in your hands and forearms.

Shoulders: Lift your shoulders towards your ears, hold, and let them drop. Feel the heaviness as they relax.

Face: Tighten your forehead, eyes, and mouth, hold, and release. Notice the smoothness across your face.

Chest and stomach: Take a deep breath, gently tighten your stomach muscles, hold, and exhale slowly as everything softens.

Legs: Press your thighs together and tense your calves, hold, and release. Feel your legs sinking into the surface beneath you.

Feet: Curl your toes downward, hold, and let them relax.

Take one more slow breath in and out. Allow your whole body to rest, loose and calm, and stay here for a moment before moving on.

SAFE PLACE VISUALISATION

Find a comfortable position, sitting or lying down. Let your hands rest naturally and close your eyes if that feels right. Take a slow breath in and release it gently. Allow your breathing to settle into a steady rhythm. Imagine a place where you feel completely safe and at ease. This might be a real location or one you create in your imagination. Picture what surrounds you in this place: the colours, the shapes, the sounds, the textures, and the scent in the air. Notice how your body responds as you rest here. Your shoulders drop, your jaw softens, and your breathing becomes smoother. If any worries appear, imagine them drifting past like clouds. You do not need to hold them right now.

Stay in this place for as long as you wish. When you are ready to return, take a deeper breath, feel the surface beneath you, and gently open your eyes.

Afterword

As you close the final pages of this book, I would like to reflect with you for a moment. Counselling, at its core, is about people, courage and facing life's challenges. I hope that all I have offered you will be of help, from practical guidance to a sense of reassurance that healing is always possible.

Writing this book has reminded me that change comes in small, steady steps, that each communication builds resolve and courage. If there is one message I wish to leave with you, it is to ask for support, embrace it and work through it with patience.

I am so grateful to the many individuals who have trusted me with their issues over the years. Their honesty, vulnerability, and strength have amazed me. They shaped the insights that you have read. To colleagues, my mentor, and to you, the reader, thank you for being part of this ongoing dialogue. As you move forward, I encourage you to continue exploring and questioning.

The last pages of this book are not an ending; they carry you forward to the beginning of your next chapter. May this book serve as a companion in moments of uncertainty, a reminder in times of struggle, and a spark of encouragement when you need it most.

www.ingramcontent.com/pod-product-compliance
Lightning Source LLC
LaVergne TN
LVHW022222200926
848481LV00006B/2084

* 9 7 8 1 8 0 7 2 3 1 4 3 9 *